Sentence Composing
11

HAYDEN WRITING SERIES

ROBERT W. BOYNTON, *Consulting Editor*

TELLING WRITING (THIRD ED.)
Ken Macrorie

WRITING TO BE READ (SECOND ED.)
Ken Macrorie

SEARCHING WRITING
Ken Macrorie

COMPOSING: WRITING AS A SELF-CREATING PROCESS
William E. Coles, Jr.

TEACHING COMPOSING
William E. Coles, Jr.

FORMING/THINKING/WRITING: THE COMPOSING IMAGINATION
Ann E. Berthoff

CONFRONT, CONSTRUCT, COMPLETE: A COMPREHENSIVE APPROACH TO WRITING
BOOKS 1 AND 2
Jack Easterling and Jack Pasanen

WRITING AT WORK: DO'S, DON'TS, AND HOW TO'S
Ernst Jacobi

WORKING AT WRITING: A WORKBOOK FOR WRITING AT WORK
Ernst Jacobi

SENTENCE COMPOSING 10
Don Killgallon

SENTENCE COMPOSING 11
Don Killgallon

SENTENCE COMPOSING 12
Don Killgallon

RHETORIC AND COMPOSITION: A SOURCEBOOK FOR TEACHERS
Richard L. Graves

EXERCISES IN READING AND WRITING
Alexandra Davis and O. B. Davis

Sentence Composing
11

DON KILLGALLON

Baltimore County Schools

HAYDEN BOOK COMPANY, INC.
Rochelle Park, New Jersey

To the person who corrected my misspellings in
Sentence Composing (and other errors elsewhere) : Mom

Selections from *A Separate Peace* by John Knowles (published by Macmillan & Co.) are reprinted by permission of Curtis Brown Ltd. Copyright © 1959 by John Knowles.

Library of Congress Cataloging in Publication Data

Killgallon, Don.
   Sentence composing 11.

   (Hayden writing series)
   Includes bibliographical references.
   SUMMARY: A textbook focusing on the composition of
sentences by using four sentence-manipulating techniques:
scrambling, imitating, combining, and expanding.
   1. English language—Sentences. 2. English language—
Composition and exercises. [1. English language—Sentences]
I. Title. II. Series.
PE1441.K48   808'.042   79-26684
ISBN 0-8104-6123-4

Printed in the United States of America

2   3   4   5   6   7   8   9   PRINTING

81 82 83 84 85 86 87 88   YEAR

Preface

This series—SENTENCE COMPOSING *10, 11,* and *12*—emphasizes the most neglected unit of written composition: the sentence. Using four sentence-manipulating techniques—*sentence scrambling, sentence imitating, sentence combining,* and *sentence expanding*—the books teach students structures they seldom use in their writing, but should and can easily use once they become familiar with them through many examples and Practices.

Each book concentrates on such structures by means of model sentences by professional writers. The rationale is based on the widely accepted mimetic theory of *oral* language acquisition, applied here to *written* language acquisition in the belief that continual exposure to structures used often by professionals in their sentences will produce attention to, understanding of, and, with practice, normal use of such structures by students in their sentences.

The books are exercises in applied grammar, with the theory and terminology of grammar subordinate to the major goal, composing sentences. The naming of parts and the parsing of sentences, the goals of traditional grammar study, are exercises in dissection. The practices in *Sentence Composing* are exercises in production.

The sentence-manipulating techniques are easily learned. The Practices based on them are interesting and challenging, and they can be done by any student. In addition, the teacher can readily give attention to the sentences students compose, with quicker, more constant, and more thorough feedback than with longer compositions.

Since the Practices have proved successful for the great majority of students who have used them in pilot programs in all kinds of schools, it is demonstrably true that *Sentence Composing* can work anywhere—in any school, with any student.

DON KILLGALLON

Baltimore, Maryland

Contents

Sentence Composing
11

Introduction: How Sentence Composing Works

The immediate goal of this textbook is to have you practice using three sentence structures that professional writers use frequently and students rarely. The ultimate goal is for you to become so familiar with these structures that you'll use them with naturalness and confidence in the sentences you compose. To help you achieve these goals, this textbook uses hundreds of professionally written model sentences, chosen because they contain these three common sentence structures.

The emphasis here is on *applied* grammar. There are few terms to learn—actually just three main ones: *absolute, appositive,* and *participle.* These terms provide a quick way to label the sentence structures you will study. Because these few terms and examples of the sentence parts they identify occur frequently, you'll have no trouble learning them.

The important thing, however, is practice in using the sentence structures to guarantee that they become a permanent part of the way you compose sentences. For this reason there are numerous varied Practices on a particular sentence structure, far more than are found in most grammar textbooks. *Sentence Composing* emphasizes practicing, not identifying; applying, not memorizing.

The method used is first to identify the particular structure, then to gain skill in using that structure, and finally to apply that skill in your own writing. Through this method, if you work well, you will learn to compose sentences in a mature style, one resembling the sentence structures used by professional writers.

The three sentence structures—absolutes, appositives, and participles— are easy to learn; to become skilled in using them, however, requires frequent practice with the many Practice exercises provided. Do not make the mistake of thinking that just because you *know* the sentence structure you will *use* it in your own writing.

Throughout this textbook you will study the sentence structures of mature writers through four easily learned techniques:

SENTENCE SCRAMBLING
SENTENCE IMITATING
SENTENCE COMBINING
SENTENCE EXPANDING

All four techniques rely upon sentences written by professional writers—*not* the articifical sentences concocted by grammar textbook editors.

SENTENCE SCRAMBLING

Sentence scrambling is the process of mixing up the parts of a sentence for you to unscramble to produce a good sentence. For example, here is a scrambled list of the sentence parts of a professionally written sentence:

1. to sit on.
2. with playing cards,
3. of the room
4. In the middle
5. and around it were grouped boxes
6. littered
7. for the players
8. stood a big square table

From a sentence by John Steinbeck, *Of Mice and Men*

PRACTICE A

Unscramble the list of sentence parts given to produce at least *two* acceptable sentences. The original is printed in the References*. Compare yours with Steinbeck's, and decide which you prefer.

---

*The section called References, in the back of the book, contains the original sentences by professional writers that were the bases for most of the Practices in this textbook. They are included so that you will have immediate feedback on how you did in the individual Practices. They should not be considered "answers in the back of the book," as in many textbooks. Strictly speaking, these are not answers. They are for comparing your sentences with the sentences of professional writers. The important thing is not whether your sentence duplicates the professional writer's, but whether you learn anything from the comparison. You may decide that the professional writer's is better; in that case, study the differences. You may decide that yours is just as good; in that case, congratulate yourself. In some cases you may decide that yours is better; in that case, take a bow. In any case, the important thing to remember is that the References are not "answers."

SENTENCE IMITATING

In sentence imitating, sentences by professional writers are used as models. The purpose is to increase your ability to vary sentence structure through deliberate imitation of the structures of the model sentences.

Model

On stormy nights, when the tide was out, the Bay of Fougere, fifty feet below the house, resembled an immense black pit, from which arose mutterings and sighs as if the sands down there had been alive and complaining.

Joseph Conrad, "The Idiots"

Imitation

During rush-hour traffic, when his nerves were frazzled, Brent Hammond, twenty miles above the speed limit, hit his brakes, from which came sharp peals and leaden grindings as though the metal were alive and hurting.

PRACTICE B

Try imitating these two models. Some sample imitations are printed in the References.

1.   He had never been hungrier, and he filled his mouth with wine, faintly tarry-tasting from the leather bag, and swallowed.

Ernest Hemingway, *For Whom the Bell Tolls*

2.   Light flickered on bits of ruby glass and on sensitive capillary hairs in the nylon-brushed nostrils of the creature that quivered gently, gently, its eight legs spidered under it on rubber-padded paws.

Ray Bradbury, *Fahrenheit 451*

SENTENCE COMBINING

In sentence combining, unlike sentence scrambling and sentence imitating, only the content is provided, not the sentence structure. You combine into a single sentence the list of reduced sentences derived from a sentence by a professional writer, and then compare your result with the original.

Reduced Sentences

1.   She returned.
2.   Her return was to her bench.
3.   Her face showed something.

4.   The something was unhappiness.

5.   The unhappiness was from all that had suddenly overtaken her.

Original

She returned to her bench, her face showing all the unhappiness that had suddenly overtaken her.

Theodore Dreiser. *An American Tragedy*

PRACTICE C

Here are three groups of reduced sentences to combine. Compare your results with the originals in the References. How do yours differ from the originals? Which do you like better? Why?

1a.   It happened in the darkness in the hallway.

b.   The hallway was by the door.

c.   The sick woman arose.

d.   In addition, she started again toward her own room.

Based on a sentence by Sherwood Anderson. *Winesburg, Ohio*

2a.   Over the fire he did something.

b.   He stuck a wire grill.

c.   He was pushing the four legs of the grill down.

d.   The legs were being pushed into the ground.

e.   He did all of this with his boot.

Based on a sentence by Ernest Hemingway, "Big Two-Hearted River: Part I"

3a.   It happened near the edge of town.

b.   The group had to walk around an automobile.

c.   The automobile was burned.

d.   In addition, the automobile was squatting.

e.   The squatting was on the narrow road.

f.   In addition, the bearers on one side fell into a deep ditch.

g.   The bearers had been unable to see their way in the darkness.

Based on a sentence by John Hersey, *Hiroshima*

SENTENCE EXPANDING

Within a reduced version of a professionally written sentence are places for you to provide additions. Here is an author's original sentence, then the reduced sentence with slash marks indicating places for additions, followed by a sample student expansion.

Original

Her eyes, lost in the fatty ridges of her face, **looked like two small pieces of coal** pressed into a lump of dough as they moved from one face to another while the visitors stated their errand.

William Faulkner, "A Rose for Emily"

Reduced Sentence

Her eyes / looked like two small pieces of coal /.

Expansion

Her eyes, **bright but dark, piercing with the intensity of their gaze,** looked like two small pieces of coal, **with an expression that suggested either high intelligence, deep malice, or both.**

Both the content and the structure of the student's additions are different from the author's sentence, but the result is an expanded sentence of equal syntactic maturity. In sentence expanding, you provide not just the content, not just the structure, but both.

PRACTICE D

For each sentence, try several expansions. The originals are printed in the References.

1. / he lived with his grandmother /.
From a sentence by Maya Angelou, *I Know Why the Caged Bird Sings*

2. / she wrote a short note to Mrs. Harvey /.
From a sentence by F. Scott Fitzgerald. "Bernice Bobs Her Hair"

You can learn much more about writing in general, not just sentence structure, through the practices in this book. In the past, the sentence has too often been neglected as a way of improving writing; instead it was used almost exclusively for analysis, with the naming of parts and parsing as the purposes. *Sentence Composing* uses the sentence as a way of improving your writing. Even though you'll be working mainly with sentences, not longer units of composition, there is much that you can learn about good writing of any length and type—paragraphs, essays, short stories, reports, research papers.

1

Punctuation and Sentence Composing

A crucial part of sentence composing is punctuation. Without it, most sentences, whether written by a professional writer or not, would be very difficult if not impossible to comprehend. This truth is easily illustrated by removing all punctuation from a sentence.

Punctuation Removed

Three figures leaned against the slanting rain Alamo Laska Nick Christopher and the boy who had run away from home.
From a sentence by Edmund Ware, "An Underground Episode"

Without punctuation, reading this sentence is a puzzling and annoying exercise. Isn't an Alamo some kind of building? But what could a "slanting rain Alamo" be? If not a building, it must be a name or part of a name; but there are four names and only "three figures" indicated. Which words go together? We could make a sensible guess, but reading shouldn't be a guessing game. We wouldn't have to ask any of these questions if the correct punctuation were included.

Punctuation Retained

Three figures leaned against the slanting rain: Alamo Laska, Nick Christopher, and the boy who had run away from home.

The value of punctuation is obvious. What is not obvious, however, is that professional writers, unlike student writers, tend to use a wider range of punctuation marks (not only commas) inside the sentences they write.

Each of the following sentences illustrates how professional writers use punctuation marks that students rarely use: semicolons, colons, and dashes.

6

1.   There was talk that her father and mother were taking her back to Earth next year; it seemed vital to her that they do so, though it would mean the loss of thousands of dollars to her family.

Ray Bradbury, "All Summer in a Day"

2.   Sweat popped out on the boy's face; he began to struggle.

Langston Hughes, "Thank You, M'am"

3.   It is more than just wind: it is a solid wall of snow moving at gale force, pounding like surf.

Richard E. Byrd, *Alone*

4.   When he reached the door, he realized what had attracted him: the smell of food.

Franz Kafka, *The Metamorphosis*

5.   Three figures leaned against the slanting rain: Alamo Laska, Nick Christopher, and the boy who had run away from home.

Edmund Ware, "An Underground Episode"

6.   The third day—it was Wednesday of the first week—Charles bounced a see-saw onto the head of a little girl and made her bleed, and the teacher made him stay inside all during recess.

Shirley Jackson, "Charles"

7.   A man with murder in his heart will murder, or be murdered—it comes to the same thing—and so I knew I had to leave.

James Baldwin, "Every Good-bye Ain't Gone"

The common element in the above sentences, uncommon in student sentences, is the use of certain punctuation marks: the semicolon (first two sentences); the colon (next three sentences); and the dash (last two sentences).

Knowing how to use these three punctuation marks opens up new possibilities for improving your sentences. It stands to reason that if you are unfamiliar with the use of certain punctuation marks, you will not use them, even when you write sentences that require them. If asked to produce three sentences—one using a semicolon, one using a colon, and one using a dash—most students would not be able to do so. Professional writers use these same marks much more frequently than students do. Obviously, professional writers know how to use them, and many students do not. The fact that expert writers choose to use them suggests that these punctuation marks make a strong contribution to good sentences. Learning them can perhaps make a strong contribution to the sentences you write and will definitely help you in working through the other parts of this text.

Sentence scrambling is an excellent way to learn. Instead of using the methods of formal grammar, sentence scrambling lists the parts of sentences containing these three punctuation marks, and you unscramble them. In this way, you become familiar with how and why authors use them. When you are familiar with the way the punctuation marks are used and secure in your ability to use them yourself, you will be able to write new and improved sentences much like those of the professional writers.

THE SEMICOLON

Here are sentences from earlier in this part of the book. Each contains a semicolon:

1.   There was talk that her father and mother were taking her back to Earth next year; it seemed vital to her that they do so, though it would mean the loss of thousands of dollars to her family.

2.   Sweat popped out on the boy's face; he began to struggle.

Each could have been written as two separate sentences.

1a.   There was talk that her father and mother were taking her back to Earth next year. It seemed vital to her that they do so, though it would mean the loss of thousands of dollars to her family.

2a.   Sweat popped out on the boy's face. He began to struggle.

Instead, the authors chose to express the content as *one sentence*, with a semicolon joining what otherwise would have been two sentences. The choice was dictated by the close interrelationship of ideas. A semicolon *signals* this interrelationship to the reader.

In theory, it's possible to join any two or more sentences simply by inserting semicolons between them. In practice, however, the number of sentences joined is rarely more than two; the two joined have what the author considers to be a strong interrelationship.

PRACTICE 1

Each of the sentences that results from unscrambling the lists of sentence parts below has a semicolon. Unscramble each list and punctuate the resulting sentences correctly. The number and type of punctuation marks in the original sentence are indicated below each list of parts. The marks indicated are used to join sentence parts. Punctuation *within* the parts (if any) is retained in the list itself.

The sentence part that should begin your unscrambled sentence is capitalized. Remember, a semicolon is the mark used to join what otherwise would have been two separate, complete sentences. When you finish, compare your work with the original sentences in the References.

Important: Do not merely list the order of the unscrambled sentence parts. Write out the complete sentence to practice using the punctuation pattern.

1a.   putting the lamp upon a low stool

b.   A few stray white bread crumbs lay

c. carrying them to his mouth one by one
d. he began to pick up the crumbs
e. on the cleanly washed floor by the table
f. with unbelievable rapidity

Punctuation: one semicolon, two commas, one period

From a sentence by Sherwood Anderson, *Winesburg, Ohio*

2a. whom Dr. Schumann remembered as having embarked
b. regarding them with what could only be described as a leer
c. A tall, shambling dark young fellow
d. at some port in Texas
e. he lounged along in the wake of the Spanish girls
f. had gone ashore
g. and was now returning

Punctuation: one semicolon, two commas, one period

From a sentence by Katherine Anne Porter, *Ship of Fools*

3a. preferring to look out on frozen cliffs
b. dirtier cars
c. it is not a pleasant corner
d. rather than dirty streets
e. of the gray Chicago winter
f. He has always wished they were on the eastern side
g. of water in the winter
h. of the building
i. in the midst

Punctuation: one semicolon, three commas, one period

From a sentence by Judith Guest, *Ordinary People*

4a. of the horses
b. from the carriage
c. For a moment Augustus thought
d. first one and then the other of the horses detached itself
e. of throwing himself in the way
f. to stop them
g. something gave way
h. but before the carriage reached him
i. and came galloping past him

Punctuation: one semicolon, two commas, one period

From a sentence by Isak Dinesen, "The Roads Round Pisa"

PRACTICE 2

Each of the items below is one half of a professionally-written sentence: the half before the semicolon or the half after the semicolon. Add content that would complete the sentence. Be sure what you add could have been a separate sentence. Because of the strong interrelationship of content with the half provided, however, you are able to join the two with a semicolon. When you have finished, compare what you added with the authors' original sentences in the References.

The number of words deleted from the original sentence is indicated. Make your addition approximately the same length.

1.   *Description of an Otter Stalking a Trout*
He came to the corner of the rock and paused, sank until his belly softly scraped the sand, and became one with the bottom's shadows; *(twelve words)*.

From a sentence by Robert Murphy, "You've Got to Learn"

2.   *Comparison of a Real Ship (the Titanic) and a Fictional Ship*
Fourteen years later a British shipping company named the White Star Line built a steamer remarkably like the one in Robertson's novel. The new liner was 66,000 tons displacement; *(four words)*. The real ship was 882.5 feet long; *(six words)*.

From sentences by Walter Lord, *A Night to Remember*

3.   *A Man Preparing to Cook Dinner*
(fifteen words); he set a kettle of water on the stove and dropped a can of beans into the water.

From a sentence by John Steinbeck, "The Snake"

4.   *Child Leaving Home for First Day of Kindergarten*
(twenty-one words); I watched him go off the first morning with the older girl next door, seeing clearly that an era of my life was ended, my sweet-voiced nursery-school tot replaced by a long-trousered swaggering character who forgot to stop at the corner and wave good-bye to me.

From a sentence by Shirley Jackson, "Charles"

THE COLON

Here are sentences from earlier in this section of the book. Each contains a colon:

1.   It is more than just a wind: it is a solid wall of snow moving at gale force, pounding like surf.

2.   When he reached the door, he realized what had attracted him: the smell of food.

3.   Three figures leaned against the slanting rain: Alamo Laska, Nick Christopher, and the boy who had run away from home.

The content to the right of the colon has a definite relationship to the content left of the colon: the right explains the left. The explanations can take one of two forms. Sometimes they are in the form of a list. In the third sentence above, for example, the list explains who the three figures were who leaned against the slanting rain. Sometimes the explanations to the right of the colon are in the form of a description of something mentioned to the left of the colon, as in the other two sentences above.

There is one important grammatical rule for writing sentences containing colons, and it applies whether the colon introduces a list or explains something to the left of the colon. *Everything to the left of the colon must be grammatically like a separate, complete sentence; if it is not, then the colon is used incorrectly.*

Read the above three sentences again. Notice that everything to the left of the colon is grammatically like a separate, complete sentence. To the right of the colon the grammatical structure varies. Such variety is common and permissible. Sometimes everything to the right is like a separate, complete sentence (#1); sometimes it is not (#2, #3). Either is acceptable.

PRACTICE 3

Each sentence below uses a colon. First, write the sentence and punctuate it. Next, tell whether the information to the right of the colon is a list, explanation, or description of something to the left of the colon. Finally, tell whether the information to the right of the colon is like a sentence or not like a sentence. (Remember, either is acceptable, provided the information to the *left* of the colon *is* like a sentence.)

1. If you walk through the museums of the world you will find a variety of instruments of torture racks thumbscrews barbed whips iron maidens pincers branding irons machines for electric shocks.
Punctuation: one colon, seven commas
From a sentence by Morris West, *The Salamander*

2. He borrowed seed sowed the land he had bought it produced well.
Punctuation: one colon, one comma
From a sentence by Leo Tolstoy, "How Much Land Does a Man Need?"

3. At the latest possible moment a bridal party appeared in a festival flurry at the foot of the gangplank a profusion of lace hats and tender-colored gauzy frocks for the women immaculate white linen and carnation buttonholes for the men.
Punctuation: one colon, two commas
From a sentence by Katherine Anne Porter, *Ship of Fools*

4. The narrow creek was like a ditch tortuous fabulously deep filled with gloom under the thin strip of pure and shining blue of the heaven.
Punctuation: one colon, two commas
From a sentence by Joseph Conrad, "The Lagoon"

PRACTICE 4

Each of the sentences that results from unscrambling the lists of sentence parts below has a colon. Unscramble the sentence and punctuate it correctly. The quantity and type of punctuation marks are indicated for each sentence; you must decide where to place them. The marks indicated are ones that join sentence parts together. Punctuation within sentence parts (if any) is retained and indicated within the list itself. The first word of the beginning sentence part is capitalized. When you finish, compare your work with the original sentences in the References.

Important: Do not merely list the order of the unscrambled sentence parts. Write out the complete sentence to practice using the punctuation pattern.

Remember, a colon is the mark used to introduce either a list, explanation, or description of something mentioned to the left of the colon.

1a. or dull

 b. himself

 c. But whether he was being brilliant

 d. he had one sole topic of conversation

Punctuation: one colon, one comma

From a sentence by Deems Taylor, "The Monster"

2a. but she is still more poised than he

 b. small, delicate features

 c. a beautiful pointed nose

 d. He has caught her off-guard

 e. the casual elegance of a painter

 f. and this close he can see her face

 g. or a dancer

Punctuation: one colon, five commas

From a sentence by Judith Guest, *Ordinary People*

3a. and much more extraordinary

 b. it is history that runs back three centuries

 c. But his real history is much longer

 d. a strange and unfathomable history

 e. than could be indicated by these flares of war

 f. into primitive America

 g. that is touched by something dark and supernatural

Punctuation: one colon, one comma

From a sentence by Thomas Wolfe, "The Men of Old Catawba"

4a. an ugly ebony African god

 b. (presented to the school by some traveling millionaire)

c. I recalled only a few cracked relics from slavery times

d. a set of ankle-irons and links of chain

e. that seemed to sneer

f. a gourd for drinking

g. an iron pot

h. an ancient bell

i. a primitive loom

j. a spinning wheel

k. a branding iron with the double letter *IV M*

l. a leather whip with copper brads

Punctuation: one colon, eight commas

From a sentence by Ralph Ellison, *Invisible Man*

PRACTICE 5

Each of the items below is one half of a professionally written sentence: the half before the colon or the half after the colon. Add content that would complete the sentence. If the problem calls for an addition before the colon, remember that what you add must be grammatically like a separate, complete sentence. If the problem calls for an addition after the colon, add the kind of content specified in the problem.

1. *An Old Man Trying to Escape*
He could never escape them, no matter how much or how far he ran: *(explanation, approximately ten words)*.

From a sentence by William Faulkner, "Wash"

2. *A River Scene Lit by Lightning*
Under the ceaseless conflagration of lightning that flamed in the skies, everything below stood out in clear-cut and shadowless distinctness: *(list of several aspects of the scene, approximately forty-seven words)*.

From a sentence by Mark Twain, *Tom Sawyer*

3. *Ransacking a Floor of a House*
They began to ransack the floor: *(list of examples of ransacking, approximately eighteen words)*.

From a sentence by James Thurber, "The Night the Ghost Got In"

4. *Series of Parallel Descriptions of Friends*

Note: Sentences containing colons are structured alike. To the left of the colon is a description of what the friends are not; to the right is a description of what the friends are. All of the sentences containing colons pattern like this: **They are not** beautiful: **they are only** decorated. The boldface words are found in each.

Your friends are all the dullest dogs I know.
They are not beautiful: they are only decorated.

They are not clean: *(approximately six words)*.
They are not dignified: *(approximately five words)*.
They are not educated: *(approximately five words)*.
They are not religious: *(approximately four words)*
They are not moral: *(approximately four words)*.

George Bernard Shaw, Man and Superman

LISTS WITH A COLON AND SEMICOLONS

Sometimes semicolons, rather than commas, are used to separate the items in a list introduced by a colon. When the items are fairly long, the list is easier to read if semicolons are used. Also, if commas are already used within the items of the list, using commas to separate one item from the next item would be confusing.

Here is an example in which some of the items in the list are fairly long, with an occasional internal comma:

He had never been to a carnival before, and everything about it thrilled him: the noise; the dust; the barrel organs grinding out the gaudy music-hall tunes; the scarlet-ribboned monkeys clambering up the arms and shoulders of the tattered music-makers, squeaking madly and pelting the laughing audience with peanuts and banana skins; the brightly colored tents with their Vanishing Lady and Madame Makura the fortune-teller and the Smallest Man in the World; the gay young girls screaming on the bumper cars in a raucous din and den of noise, their wide-flared summer dresses flung high by the onrush of air; the boys and young men laughing and winking and making obscene signs with their fingers.

Christy Brown, Down All the Days

PRACTICE 6

Copy and punctuate correctly each of the following sentences. All of them contain lists that must be introduced with a colon. The lists themselves, however, require one of two types of punctuation. If the items in the list are short with no commas within them, separate them with commas. If the items are fairly long or contain commas, separate them with semicolons.

1.　In two respects it was an exceptionally safe car: first, it didn't go very fast second, it had three foot pedals. . . .

E. B. White, "From Sea to Shining Sea"

2.　There were all the human smells too of the hundreds of people who filled the boardwalk: ladies in print dresses smelling like passing gardens swimmers with their scents of sun-tan oils and skin lotions. . . .

Jessamyn West, Cress Delahanty

3.　*The Martian Chronicles* makes use of a dozen or more stock ingredients of pulp science-fiction: mental telepathy materialized fantasies robots mass hypnosis intersecting time-planes super-creatures made of blue phosphorous light. . . .

Clifton Fadiman, "Prefatory Note," *The Martian Chronicles*

4.   The little flotilla then set out across the uncharted San Francisco Bay: Sutter, with his title of captain which he had invented in the same manner that he had conjured up his role of empire builder the eight Kanaka men and two Kanaka women who had contracted to stay with him for three years and help build his settlement a fourteen-year-old Indian boy whom he had bought for $100 in the Wind River Rendezvous a German cabinetmaker three recruits from Yerba Buena and several sailors on the beach.

Irving Stone, *Men to Match My Mountains*

5.   We hold these truths to be self-evident: that all men are created equal that they are endowed by their Creator with certain inalienable rights that among these are life, liberty, and the pursuit of happiness that to secure these rights, governments are instituted among men, deriving their just powers from the consent of the governed that whenever any form of government becomes destructive of these ends, it is the right of the people to alter or abolish it, and to institute a new government, laying its foundation on such principles, and organizing its powers in such forms, as to them shall seem most likely to effect their safety and happiness.

Thomas Jefferson, *The Declaration of Independence*

REVIEW OF SEMICOLON AND COLON

PRACTICE 7

Decide what punctuation mark is needed in the blank represented by the letter in parentheses: a semicolon, a colon, or a comma. Be prepared to explain your choice.

1.   The mountains were miles away from the house of the family, and sometimes they were altogether hidden by weather (A) cloud (B) or rain (C) or wind alive with dust.

From a sentence by Paul Horgan, "To the Mountains"

2.   In two respects it was an exceptionally safe car (A) first (B) it didn't go very fast (C) second (D) it had three foot pedals. . . .

From a sentence by E. B. White, "From Sea to Shining Sea"

3.   Sometimes he was brilliant (A) sometimes he was maddeningly tiresome. But whether he was being brilliant or dull, he had one sole topic of conversation (B) himself.

From sentences by Deems Taylor, "The Monster"

4.   There were two moons (A) a clock moon with four faces in four night directions above the solemn black courthouse (B) and the real moon that was slowly rising in vanilla whiteness from the dark east.

From a sentence by Ray Bradbury, "The Whole Town's Sleeping"

5.　"Crazy-looking thing," we would chime in; crazy meant anything wrong, anything different from the norm, which was, of course, Geraldine herself (A) pig-tailed (B) gingham-dressed (C) belted at the hipline (D) scornful (E) *right*.

From a sentence by Nancy Hale, "You Never Know"

6.　We had a dispute whether the rider had to be on his horse at the finish, and it happened so often that the horse came in alone that we made a rule (A) a horse (B) with or without his rider (C) won or lost the race.

From a sentence by Lincoln Steffens, "A Boy on Horseback"

7.　He then goes on to describe this "weede or plante" in considerable detail (A) its leaves are broad and coarse, and when dried it is yellow and has a strong odor.

From a sentence by Thomas Wolfe, "The Men of Old Catawba"

8.　In the next day Koona went, and but five of them remained (A) Pike (B) crippled and limping (C) only half conscious and not conscious enough longer to malinger (D) Sol-leks (E) the one-eyed, still faithful to the toil of trace and trail (F) and mournful in that he had so little strength with which to pull (G) Teek (H) who had not travelled so far that winter and who was now beaten more than the others because he was fresher (I) and Buck (J) still at the head of the team (K) but no longer enforcing discipline or striving to enforce it (L) blind with weakness half the time and keeping the trail by the loom of it and by the dim feel of his feet.

From a sentence by Jack London, *Call of the Wild*

PRACTICE 8

Write three sentences containing semicolons. Write six sentences containing colons, three introducing lists and three introducing explanations. Write three long sentences with colons introducing lists, each long item in the list separated from the next item with a semicolon.

THE DASH

Here are sentences from earlier in this part of the book. Each contains a dash:

1.　The third day—it was Wednesday of the first week—Charles bounced a see-saw onto the head of a little girl and made her bleed, and the teacher made him stay inside all during recess.

2.　A man with murder in his heart will murder, or be murdered—it comes to the same thing—and so I knew I had to leave.

The dashes indicate parenthetical information that interrupts the flow of the sentence. Strictly speaking, the material enclosed inside the dashes is not grammatically related to the rest of the sentence; if the material were removed, the rest of the sentence would be grammatically intact.

1a. The third day Charles bounced a see-saw onto the head of a little girl and made her bleed, and the teacher made him stay inside all during recess.

2a. A man with murder in his heart will murder, or be murdered, and so I knew I had to leave.

PRACTICE 9

Each of the sentences that results from unscrambling the lists of sentence parts below has dashes. Unscramble the sentence and punctuate it correctly. The number and type of punctuation marks contained in the original sentence are indicated. The marks are ones that join or separate sentence parts. Punctuation *within* the parts (if any) is retained in the list itself.

The sentence part that should begin your unscrambled sentence is capitalized. Remember, a dash is the mark used to indicate an interruption within the sentence.

Important: Do not merely list the order of the unscrambled sentence parts. Write out the complete sentence to practice the punctuation pattern.

1a. where a collection of cloth samples was scattered
  b. and had put in a pretty gilded frame.
  c. Over the table
  d. Samsa was a commercial traveler
  e. that he had recently cut from an illustrated paper
  f. hung the picture
Punctuation: two dashes, one comma, one period
From a sentence by Franz Kafka, *The Metamorphosis*

2a. the complex, the inexplicable
  b. of the inferior man
  c. The one permanent emotion
  d. fear of the unknown
  e. as of all simpler mammals
  f. is fear
Punctuation: one dash, three commas, one period
From a sentence by H. L. Mencken, "American Culture"

3a. of exactly my own age
  b. And a man
  c. and offered me his seat
  d. he was a little older
  e. or perhaps
  f. got up
Punctuation: two dashes, one period
From a sentence by Dylan Thomas, *Quite Early One Morning*

4a. between each pair of capes
b. of the rhythmically swirling waters
c. Each is a cusp
d. of the Gulf Stream eddies
e. projecting seaward
f. in a long curving arc
g. the beach runs
h. the expression

Punctuation: one dash, one semicolon, one period

From a sentence by Rachel L. Carson, *The Sea around Us*

PRACTICE 10

Each of the items below is a sentence from which the content requiring the dash has been omitted. Add content that would complete the sentence. Remember that what you add must interrupt the flow of the sentence. When you finish, compare what you added with the authors' original sentences in the References.

The number of words deleted from the original sentence is indicated. Make your addition approximately the same length.

1. *Resemblances among the Men*
At first he thought the men all looked alike—*(eight words)*—and then he saw the man with the yellow eyes.

From a sentence by A. B. Guthrie, "First Principal"

2. *Description of the Landscape*
Compared with this gridwork, the natural landscape—*(ten words)*—just can't quite catch your attention.

From a sentence by Wolfgang Langewiesche, *A Flier's World*

3. *Method for Getting His Body Out of Bed*
When Gregor had half his body out of bed—*(twenty-one words)*—he began to think how easily he could have got up if only he had had a little assistance.

From a sentence by Franz Kafka, *The Metamorphosis*

4. *Description of the Speech*
You want to be head of the class, valedictorian, so you can make a speech on Graduation Day—*(eight words)*—and be the boy wonder of the school.

From a sentence by John Knowles, *A Separate Peace*

PRACTICE 11

Write five sentences, each containing dashes. Vary the length and structure of the content set off by the dashes, sometimes using only a few words and sometimes, many.

REVIEW

In the following Practice you'll be using the punctuation skills you acquired in this section. You'll have to decide which marks—semicolons, colons, dashes, commas—are appropriate.

PRACTICE 12

Make sentences of each scrambled list below and punctuate correctly. The type of punctuation is indicated below each list, but you must decide where to place each mark. The marks indicated are ones that join or separate sentence parts. Punctuation *within* the parts (if any) is retained in the list itself.

The sentence part that should begin your unscrambled sentence is capitalized. When you finish, compare your work with the original sentences in the References.

Important: Do not merely list the order of the unscrambled sentence parts. Write out the complete sentence to practice using the punctuation pattern.

1a. of Mencken
  b. concluding with one hot, short sentence
  c. The article was a furious denunciation
  d. Mencken is a fool.
Punctuation: one colon, one comma, one period

From a sentence by Richard Wright, *Black Boy*

2a. eating what you wanted
  b. if you wanted
  c. It was a great luxury
  d. sleeping all day
Punctuation: one colon, one comma, one period

From a sentence by Mary Gordon, *Final Payments*

3a. and her brother Bill
  b. For her pallbearers
  c. her Latin teacher, W. L. Holtz
  d. her friend, W. H. Finney
  e. her pal at the "Gazette" office, Walter Hughes
  f. her high school principal, Rice Brown
  g. only her friends were chosen
  h. her doctor, Frank Foncannon
Punctuation: one colon, five semicolons, one period

From a sentence by William Allen White, "Mary White"

4a. and something called "guts" or "character"

  b. to impose your will on others

  c. It was not only money

  d. there were also strength, beauty, charm, athleticism

  e. that mattered

  f. which in reality meant the power

Punctuation: one colon, two commas, one period
From a sentence by George Orwell, "Such, Such Were the Joys"

5a. who existed

  b. in the world

  c. He was not only the most important person

  d. he was the only person

  e. in his own eyes

  f. to himself

Punctuation: one semicolon, one comma, one period
From a sentence by Deems Taylor, "The Monster"

6a. that from these honored dead we take increased devotion

  b. to the great task remaining before us

  c. It is rather for us to be here dedicated

  d. shall not perish from the earth

  e. by the people

  f. that this nation, under God, shall have a new birth of freedom

  g. and for the people

  h. and that government of the people

  i. to that cause for which they gave the last full measure of devotion

  j. that these dead shall not have died in vain

  k. that we here highly resolve

Punctuation: one dash, three semicolons, three commas, one period
From a sentence by Abraham Lincoln, "The Gettysburg Address"

7a. and it is strictly an air sight

  b. North–South and East–West

  c. It is really one of the odd sights of the world

  d. and I mean precisely

  e. in a mathematical gridwork

  f. lined up in endless lanes that run precisely

  g. exact, straight-sided

  h. a whole country laid out

  i. in sections one mile square each

Punctuation: one colon, two dashes, three commas, one period
From a sentence by Wolfgang Langewiesche, *A Flier's World*

2

Sentence Composing
with Absolute Phrases

IDENTIFYING THE SKILL

Here is a list of sentences, all of which were written by professional writers. However, some parts have been deleted.

1.   She returned to her bench.
2.   The boy watched.
3.   About the bones, ants were ebbing away.
4.   Six boys came over the hill half an hour early that afternoon, running hard.

Now compare the above sentences with the originals. Notice that the part deleted, when combined with the reduced sentence above, accounts for the distinctiveness of the author's original sentence.

1a.   She returned to her bench, **her face showing all the unhappiness that had suddenly overtaken her.**
Theodore Dreiser, An American Tragedy

2a.   The boy watched, **his eyes bulging in the dark.**
Edmund Ware, "An Underground Episode"

3a.   About the bones, ants were ebbing away, **their pincers full of meat.**
Doris Lessing, African Stories

4a.   Six boys came over the hill half an hour early that afternoon, running hard, **their heads down, their forearms working, their breath whistling**.
John Steinbeck, The Red Pony

The boldface phrases are absolute phrases, one of the sentence parts that differentiate professional writing from student writing. They are frequently used by professional writers but are rarely used by students. Absolute phrases are an efficient way to combine related ideas in one sentence.

CHARACTERISTICS OF ABSOLUTE PHRASES

Definition

An absolute phrase is a modifier that grammatically resembles a complete sentence. Included in every absolute phrase is a subject and a partial verb, which is why it resembles a complete sentence. However, since the verb is only partial and not complete, absolutes are considered phrases and not clauses. Missing in every absolute phrase is an auxiliary verb—almost always a form of the verb *to be* (*is, are, was,* or *were*). Here are examples of absolute phrases with auxiliary verbs inserted (in parentheses) that would transform the phrase into a complete sentence (main clause). The absolute phrases are taken from the above four sentences.

1a. Her face (was) showing all the unhappiness that had suddenly overtaken her.

2a. His eyes (were) bulging in the dark.

3a. Their pincers (were) full of meat.

4a. Their heads (were) down. Their forearms (were) working. Their breath (was) whistling.

Another distinguishing characteristic of the great majority of absolute phrases is the kind of word they usually begin with. In all of the absolute phrases above, a possessive pronoun is the starting word:

1a. *her*

2a. *his*

3a. *their*

4a. *their*

The class of words called possessive pronouns has only a few members: *my, your, his, her, its, our,* and *their.* In absolute phrases the possessive pronoun is usually stated, but sometimes it is implied. In the first sentence below, the possessive pronoun that starts the absolute phrase is stated; in the second, it is implied.

Stated

Noiselessly Lenny appeared in the open doorway and stood there looking in, **his** big shoulders nearly filling the opening.

John Steinbeck, *Of Mice and Men*

Implied

The good dogs came stiffly out of their little houses, [their] hackles up and deep growls in their throats.

John Steinbeck, *The Red Pony*

In summary, there are two ways to identify absolute phrases: (1) the phrase could be transformed into a sentence by adding an auxiliary verb—usually *was* or *were*— and (2) frequently, but not always, the starting word in the absolute phrase is a possessive pronoun, stated or implied.

Position

An absolute phrase can be used as a sentence opener (precedes a clause), S-V split (splits the subject and verb of a clause), or sentence closer (follows a clause).

Punctuation

When the absolute phrase is a sentence opener (introductory position), a comma follows it.

His head aching, his throat sore, he forgot to light the cigarette.

Sinclair Lewis, Cass Timberlane

When the absolute phrase is an S-V split (intermediate position), commas precede and follow it.

Miss Hearne, **her face burning,** hardly listened to these words.

Brian Moore, The Lonely Passion of Judith Hearne

When the absolute phrase is a sentence closer (terminal position), a comma precedes the phrase and a period follows it.

Light flickered on bits of ruby glass and on sensitive capillary hairs in the nylon-brushed nostrils of the creature that quivered gently, gently, **its eight legs spidered under it on rubber-padded paws.**

Ray Bradbury, Fahrenheit 451

PRACTICE 1

Each of the professionally written sentences below contains an absolute phrase. For each sentence, do the following:

(a)   Identify the absolute phrase and test your identification by transforming the phrase into a complete sentence by adding the appropriate auxiliary verb (*was* or *were*).

(b)   Indicate the possessive pronoun that starts the absolute phrase. Where the possessive pronoun is implied rather than stated, state the intended pronoun.

(c)   State the position of the absolute phrase (sentence opener, S-V split, sentence closer).

(d)   Punctuate the absolute phrase correctly.

1.   High in the air, a little figure his hands thrust in his short jacket pockets stood staring out to sea.

Katherine Mansfield, "The Voyage"

2.   He walked with a prim strut, swinging out his legs in a half-circle with each step his heels biting smartly into the red velvet carpet on the floor.

Carson McCullers, "The Jockey"

3.   Outside, his carpetbag in his hand he stood for a time in the barnyard.

Jessamyn West, "A Time of Learning"

4.   Freddy Malins clambered in after her and spent a long time settling her on the seat Mr. Browne helping him with advice.

James Joyce, "The Dead"

5.   Father lay crumped up on the stone floor of the pantry face down arms twisted at a curious angle. . . .

Christy Brown, Down All the Days

PRACTICING THE SKILL: SENTENCE SCRAMBLING

Practice flexibility in the positioning of absolute phrases in the sentences you compose. Remember, an absolute phrase may occur in any of three positions.

Sentence Opener (Introductory)

His eyes bulging in the dark, the boy watched.

S-V Split (Intermediate)

The boy, **his eyes bulging in the dark,** watched.

Sentence Closer (Terminal)

The boy watched, **his eyes bulging in the dark.**

Sometimes the positions are interchangeable, as illustrated above. Which of the three positions to use will depend on such things as sentence variety, the relative emphasis desired, and the relationship between the structure and content of the sentence and the other sentences in the paragraph.

Sometimes ony two of the three positions are options; the third would result in unacceptable grammar, poor modification, or lack of emphasis. In the repositionings below, the intermediate position is inferior to the introductory or terminal positions because the juxtaposition of *he* and *his* sounds unpleasant.

Introductory

His long matted beard and hair gray to nearly white, he was an old man.

Intermediate (Unacceptable)

He, **his long matted beard and hair gray to nearly white,** was an old man.

Terminal

He was an old man, **his long matted beard and hair gray to nearly white.**
Walter Van Tilburg Clark, "The Portable Phonograph"

Sometimes only one of the three positions may be used effectively; the other two would result in unacceptable grammar, poor modification, or lack of emphasis. In the repositionings below, only the terminal position is acceptable.

Introductory (Unacceptable)

Its site marked by an ancient and ramshackled cabin, dying men, clinching their testimony with nuggets that were unlike any known grade of gold in the Northland, had sworn the mine existed.

Intermediate (Unacceptable)

Dying men, **its site marked by an ancient and ramshackled cabin,** clinching their testimony with nuggets that were unlike any known grade of gold in the Northland, had sworn the mine existed.

Terminal

Dying men, clinching their testimony with nuggets that were unlike any known grade of gold in the Northland, had sworn the mine existed, **its site marked by an ancient and ramshackled cabin.**
Jack London, *Call of the Wild*

PRACTICE 2

Unscramble each list of sentence parts three times: first to produce a sentence with the absolute phrase in the introductory position; next, in the intermediate position; and finally, in the terminal position. Classify the use of each position as either acceptable or unacceptable. If two (or all three) positions are acceptable, discuss which position you prefer. Punctuate correctly.

1a. had already disappointed him
 b. the park
 c. its amusements a mere glimmer of Palisades or Coney Island
 d. formal, unlovely
From a sentence by Brian Moore, *The Lonely Passion of Judith Hearne*

2a. was awake for quite a long time
 b. the moonlight on her face
 c. thinking about things
 d. I
 e. and watching Catherine sleeping
From a sentence by Ernest Hemingway, *A Farewell to Arms*

3a. each child carrying his little bag of crackling

b. we

c. in the cold winter afternoon

d. trod the long road home

e. one of many small groups of children

From a sentence by Peter Abrahams, *Tell Freedom*

4a. I

b. each set upon a carved wooden base

c. looked across to a lighted case of Chinese design

d. which held delicate-looking statues

e. of horses and birds, small vases and bowls

From a sentence by Ralph Ellison, *Invisible Man*

A sentence may contain more than one absolute phrase. When it contains two or more consecutive absolutes, they are called "compound."

Examples of Compound Absolute Phrases

We were sitting in the deep leather chairs, **the champagne in the ice-bucket** and **our glasses on the table between us**.

Ernest Hemingway, *A Farewell to Arms*

The two absolute phrases by Hemingway are joined by the coordinating conjunction *and*.

Mariko was still on her knees in one corner of the next room, **a livid welt on her cheek, her hair disheveled, her kimono in tatters, bad bruises on her thighs and lower back**.

James Clavell, *Shogun*

Here the four consecutive absolute phrases are joined with commas.

PRACTICE 3

Each of the scrambled sentences below contains compound absolute phrases. Unscramble each sentence to produce the most effective arrangement of the sentence parts. Punctuate correctly. When you finish, compare your sentence with the original in the References. How does yours differ? Which do you like better? Why?

1a. while Buck struggled in fury

b. then the rope tightened mercilessly

c. and his great chest panting

d. his tongue lolling out of his mouth

From a sentence by Jack London, *Call of the Wild*

2a.   wherever it settled its weight

b.   it ran

c.   its taloned feet clawing damp earth

d.   leaving prints six inches deep

e.   its pelvic bones crushing aside trees and bushes
From a sentence by Ray Bradbury, "A Sound of Thunder"

3a.   her shoulders drooping a little

b.   her glasses winking in the sunlight

c.   she was now standing

d.   arms akimbo

e.   her head cocked to one side
From a sentence by Harper Lee, *To Kill a Mockingbird*

4a.   as if he could squeal or laugh out loud

b.   and then

c.   his hand in one pocket clutching the money

d.   he felt

e.   his feet sinking in the soft nap of the carpet
From a sentence by Theodore Dreiser, *An American Tragedy*

5a.   you could hear the signs and murmurs as the furthest chambers of it died

b.   within

c.   closing up forever

d.   the organs malfunctioning

e.   everything shutting off

f.   liquids running a final instant from pocket to sac to spleen
From a sentence by Ray Bradbury, "A Sound of Thunder"

6a.   eyes closed

b.   just behind him

c.   and jostled a light wheel chair along

d.   with weak dark whiskers flecked with gray

e.   a tall boy with glittering golden hair and a sulky mouth pushed

f.   his spread hands limp on the brown rug over his knees

g.   in which sat a small weary dying man
From a sentence by Katherine Ann Porter, *Ship of Fools*

7a.   by the back-flung front door

b.   we had long thought of them

c.   and clutching a horsewhip

d.   as a tableau

e.   the two of them framed

f.   Miss Emily a slender figure in white in the background

g.   in the foreground
h.   her father a spraddled silhouette
i.   his back to her

From a sentence by William Faulkner, "A Rose for Emily"

PRACTICING THE SKILL: SENTENCE IMITATING

Here is an exceptionally long sentence from *A Farewell to Arms* by Ernest Hemingway. In the section of the novel from which it is taken, the narrator, Lt. Henry, is describing a vista in Switzerland. He uses compound absolute phrases, each one adding to the layered description of the scene:

Then along the road we passed an old square-built stone chateau on a ledge on the side of the mountain-side with the terraced fields of vines, each vine tied to a stick to hold it up, the vines dry and brown, and the earth ready for the snow, and the lake down below flat and gray as steel.

The compound absolute phrases are all in the terminal position (following the main clause of the sentence). Compare the following sentence with the one by Hemingway:

Finally in the kitchen we packed the wicker picnic basket with the foods for the afternoon at the harbor festival of yachting, on the bottom vegetables wrapped in cellophane to preserve them, the vegetables crisp and fresh, and the salad ready for the dressing, and the hamburger on top of the vegetables stacked and shaped in patties.

This sentence imitates the structure of Hemingway's. Like Hemingway's sentence, it contains compound absolute phrases in the terminal position.

PRACTICE 4

Underneath the model sentence are three imitations. Both the model and the imitations contain absolute phrases. The imitations are presented as a list of scrambled sentence parts for you to unscramble to duplicate the structure of the model. The first imitation, for content, uses nonsense language that will help you focus your attention on only structural similarities between the scrambled sentence and the model. The two other imitations use sense language. Unscramble each of the three sentences to produce a sentence similar in structure to the model. In addition, identify the sentence part in the scrambled list that is the absolute phrase.

Model

The motorcycle on the sidewalk speeded up and skidded obliquely into a plate-glass window, the front wheel bucking and climbing the brick base beneath the window.

Frank Rooney, "Cyclist's Raid"

Scrambled Nonsense Imitation

1a. and blatted nignly

b. its back teeth slamting and gorgling the steamed brick under the oven

c. a fermile with a pencil grooged down

d. toward a wind-swept stapler

Scrambled Sense Imitation

2a. the other customers rallying and demanding the same reduction in the cost

b. one customer in the line spoke out

c. about the unfair price

d. and ranted continuously

Scrambled Sense Imitation

3a. and moved quickly

b. one couple heading and leading the rest through the complicated steps

c. into two lines

d. several dancers near the band joined together

PRACTICE 5

Here the model sentence is broken into the four sentence parts that you un-scrambled, arranged in the same order in which they occur in the model. For each part from the model, list the equivalent part from each of the scrambled versions. After providing the equivalent parts, write two of your own sentences imitating the model, one sentence part at a time.

First Sentence Part

Model: **The motorcycle on the sidewalk speeded up**

Second Sentence Part

Model: **and skidded obliquely**

Third Sentence Part

Model: **into a plate-glass window,**

Fourth Sentence Part (Absolute Phrase)

Model: **the front wheel bucking and climbing the brick base beneath the window.**

PRACTICE 6

This Practice will review absolute phrases as well as provide examples of imitations of models. Later Practices, in which you do the imitating, will be easier for having done this exercise.

First, read the model carefully, paying special attention to the structure: position, type, and number of sentence parts; punctuation; and so forth. Next, read through the three sentences underneath the model and, again paying special attention to the parts of each of the three sentences, identify the one sentence that is an imitation of the model.

This Practice contains nonsense language that will make it easier for you to focus primarily on the *way* and not the *what* of the sentence: the structure, not the content.

In each model the absolute phrase is in boldface.

1. *Model:* They beetered by the farner, **the tangerine crimping a sock with its tendril and groosing it some weemert jolgs inside**.

A. They cransted and forsted, a fine bit of sugary clam, mustering over the filmious banad, with never a trice of zoogurd.

B. We zithered along the apple, the greaser noodling a farner with his yoogurt and vanting it many times ago.

C. After the coffee, its cumnert over-padded, escaped the sangling pevor, its handle becoomed a very light surg three times.

2. *Model:* Cravert sooned near it, **a blank bedused look on his elbow**, because Stradnem wrote with the ashtray to hear of the bookend.

A. He leaped the mert, a square apple with noots, and danced, blinging the yellow tree, near the brook for nine needles.

B. Pringing zveltly over the brocaded boom, a bear sleeping nearby, he began to sew the oven interior with green spaghetti.

C. They blazoned about it, a red happy expression on their chairs, while the woodt leaned over the table to zoozle in the nap.

3. *Model:* Around there, the runner, in his two chocolates, verned small and wide in the green grape, **the tracks of his five smabbles pinking like those of a fernid twinkled blouse with a large button**.

A. Over yonder, the bicycle, with its gramious needles, warted high and low through the dark sunshine, the sides of its big blisters starking barryingly like two of the darkened gingerbread fence near glasses.

B. Noontime, the seeker, his two chocolates running, grappled below, greeping the felangers, the bleats, and the mandanders, all of which carpted once, twice, thrice, with narry a tarry, hardly a bardly.

C.   Around three, the blandit, a tall, thin pencil, tortled howly and wide like a tined feather, and the sides of his lighter were wrinkling dryly amid funny fires of hot ice, splashed by smoke.

If you were able to pick out the imitation of the model, you saw that structure, like content, is something that you can *read.* Noticing structure, both in the sentences of professional writers and in your own, is an important skill to develop—one that will help you write mature sentences easily.

PRACTICE 7

Now that you are familiar with the structure of the model sentences from the previous Practice, your work here will be simple. In this Practice, write two sentence imitations for each of the three models in the previous Practice, using their sentence structure but providing your own content.

Each sentence below is the original of the nonsense models in the last Practice. First, tell which sentence matches which model. Then, write two imitations: a nonsense imitation and a sense imitation. The absolute phrases are in boldface.

1.   Mary Jane gazed after her, **a moody puzzled expression on her face,** while Mrs. Conroy leaned over the banisters to listen for the hall-door.
James Joyce, "The Dead"

2.   We rowed along the shore, **the barman holding the line in his hand and giving it occasional jerks forward.**
Ernest Hemingway, *A Farewell to Arms*

3.   Over yonder, the Schenley, in its vacant stretch, loomed big and square through the fine rain, **the windows of its twelve stories glowing like those of a lighted cardboard house under a Christmas tree.**
Willa Cather, "Paul's Case"

PRACTICE 8

In this last Practice on sentence imitating using absolute phrases, you can test your ability to imitate model sentences without any aid other than the model.

The model sentences are arranged in three groups according to the position of the absolute phrase. Following the structure of the model sentence, but using your own content, write a sentence imitation for each of the models below. Imitate the structure of the entire sentence, not just the absolute phrase.

Introductory Absolute Phrases (Sentence Openers)

1.   Outside, **his carpetbag in his hand,** he stood for a time in the barnyard.
Jessamyn West, "A Time of Learning"

2.   His head aching, his throat sore, he forgot to light the cigarette.

Sinclair Lewis, *Cass Timberlane*

3. A moment later, **his hands upraised, his pony's bridle reins caught in the crook of one arm,** a young man moved into the zone of light that shone bravely out through Tim Geogehan's back window.

F. R. Buckley, "Gold-Mounted Guns"

Intermediate Absolute Phrases (S-V Splits)

4. A seared man, **his charred clothes fuming where the blast had blown out the fire,** rose from the curb.

Fritz Leiber, "A Bad Day for Sales"

5. Some got out, **their bodies burnt and flattened,** and went off not knowing where they were going.

Ernest Hemingway, *A Farewell to Arms*

6. Mammoth Mister Victor Mature, **sweat streaming down his face,** met and held the lion, bigger now as the close-up showed its mammoth jaws, its mammoth fangs.

Brian Moore, *The Lonely Passion of Judith Hearne*

Terminal Absolute Phrases (Sentence Closers)

7. A water snake slipped along on the pool, **its head held up like a little periscope.**

John Steinbeck, *Of Mice and Men*

8. Jack stood up as he said this, **the bloodied knife in his hands.**

William Golding, *Lord of the Flies*

9. My brother came to my side, **his eyes drawn by the blazing straws.**

Richard Wright, *Native Son*

PRACTICING THE SKILL: SENTENCE COMBINING

In this part you'll produce single sentences from lists derived from sentences by professional writers. Each of the original sentences contains an absolute phrase. In the References are the originals for you to compare with yours. In sentence combining you have to make more choices about sentence structure than you did in sentence imitating. Here, you must decide what form or structure to give the list of sentences as you combine them into just one sentence.

PRACTICE 9

In one of the sentences in each group, a slash mark (/) indicates that the original sentence has an absolute phrase at that place. Combine the sentences underneath into an absolute phrase that will fit smoothly into the place. Write an imitation of the resulting sentence, using your own content and the structure of the model. For example:

Sentence One: She slid back the roof of the cockpit once again, / .
Sentence Two: Her nose was wrinkling.
Sentence Three: It was wrinkling at the rankness of the morass.
Sentence Four: The morass was dripping.
Sentence Five: The morass was encircling them.

Combination with Absolute Phrase

She slid back the roof of the cockpit once again, **her nose wrinkling at the rankness of the dripping morass encircling them.**
Alan Dean Foster, "Splinter of the Mind's Eye"

Imitation

He climbed down the limb of the cherry tree very slowly, **his arms tightening around the bark of the big branch supporting him.**

1a. The town lay on a broad estuary, / .
b. The town's old yellow plastered buildings were hugging something.
c. The buildings were hugging the beach.
Based on a sentence by John Steinbeck, *The Pearl*

2a. Like giants they toiled, / .
b. The days were flashing on the heels of days like dreams.
c. This happened as they heaped the treasure up.
Based on a sentence by Jack London, *Call of the Wild*

3a. In solid phalanxes the leaders crowded about the three jaguars, / , / . (two absolute phrases)
b. Their tusks were thrust.
c. The thrusting was forward.
d. Their little eyes were bloodshot with anger.
e. In addition, they were bloodshot with battle lust.
Based on a sentence by Tom Gill, "Jungle War"

4a. An Arab on a motorcycle, / , passed John at such a clip that the spirals of dust from his turnings on the winding road looked like little tornadoes.
b. The Arab's robes were flying.
c. The robes were long.
d. The robes were flying in the wind.
e. The wind was of his speed.
Based on a sentence by Elizabeth Yates, "Standing in Another's Shoes"

PRACTICE 10

Below you are given a model sentence and then a list of sentences to be combined to resemble the structure of the model. In addition to practicing the use of absolute phrases, you will practice other sentence composing skills used by the authors of the model sentences. You may not know the names of the other skills, but you will be able to imitate them if you follow the directions for this Practice. The names aren't important; your use of the skills is.

First, read the model several times, paying special attention to the structure of the sentence. In each model the absolute phrase is in boldface. Study it. Also, study the rest of the sentence carefully; you'll need to be familiar with not only the absolute phrase but also the rest of the sentence structure.

Next, read the list of sentences underneath the model. Combine these into one sentence having basically the same structure as the model. The order in which the sentences are listed is the order of the parts of the model. In other words, convert the first sentence into the first sentence part of the model, the second sentence into the second part, and so forth.

Finally, write an imitation of the model, keeping the same structure but providing your own content. For example:

Model

He returned, shuddering, five minutes later, **his arms soaked and red to the elbows**.

Ray Bradbury, "A Sound of Thunder"

Sentences to Be Converted	Conversions
1. This is about the soldiers.	1. The soldiers
2. They retreated.	2. retreated,
3. They were shivering.	3. shivering,
4. This happened two days ago.	4. two days ago,
5. Their spirits were outraged.	5. their spirits outraged
6. In addition, their spirits were crushed.	6. and crushed
7. This effect on their spirits was caused by the defeat.	7. by the defeat.

Imitation

She left, smiling, a minute before, **her Andrew Wyeth print matted and framed in green**.

Here are the three sentences with their equivalent sentence parts:

Model	Combination	Imitation
1. He	1. The soldiers	1. She
2. returned,	2. retreated,	2. left,

3. shuddering,	3. shivering,	3. smiling,
4. five minutes later,	4. two days ago,	4. a minute before,
5. his arms soaked	5. their spirits outraged	5. her Andrew Wyeth print matted
6. and red	6. and crushed	6. and framed
7. to the elbows.	7. by the defeat.	7. in green.

Here are the three sentences from this example: same structure, different content. Absolute phrases are in boldface.

Model

He returned, shuddering, five minutes later, **his arms soaked and red to the elbows**.

Combination

The soldiers retreated, shivering, two days ago, **their spirits outraged and crushed by the defeat**.

Imitation

She left, smiling, a minute before, **her Andrew Wyeth print matted and framed in green**.

Convert one sentence at a time into a structure resembling the equivalent part of the model sentence. Continue until you have converted all the sentences into the structures of equivalent parts of the model sentence.

A. *Model*: The electric train was there waiting, **all the lights on**.
Ernest Hemingway, A Farewell to Arms

1. The youngest brother was nearby.
2. He was resting.
3. All his work was over.

B. *Model*: As soon a she was well, we went to Southend-on-the-Sea for a holiday, **Mother outfitting us completely with new clothes**.
Charles Spencer Chaplin (Charlie Chaplin), My Autobiography

1. It happened as soon as it was over.
2. What happened then was that they pranced around Gracie.
3. They did their prancing like courtiers.
4. Paul was wooing her disgustingly.
5. He wooed her with his stretched smiles.

C.   *Model*: Then, very afraid, she shook her head warningly, and touched a finger to her lips and shook her head again, **her eyes pleading with him**.

James Clavell, *Shogun*

1.   Later, he was somewhat sorry.
2.   He held the baby.
3.   He held it soothingly.
4.   In addition, he brought the music box to her.
5.   He wound the toy up.
6.   His voice was singing with it.

D.   *Model*: The old woman pointed upwards interrogatively and, on my aunt's nodding, proceeded to toil up the narrow staircase before us, **her bowed head being scarcely above the level of the banister-rail**.

James Joyce, "The Sisters"

1.   The student teacher erased everything quickly.
2.   In addition, she did something with a hurried cover-up.
3.   She started to call out the spelling words.
4.   She did this for us.
5.   Her embarrassment was definitely coming from something.
6.   It was coming from her misspelling.
7.   The misspelling was on the chalkboard.

PRACTICE 11

Combine each list of sentences into one sentence containing an absolute phrase. Underline each phrase. You may eliminate words and change their form as long as the intended meaning remains. Punctuate correctly. When you finish, compare your sentences with the originals in the References.

1a.   I could hear him.
b.   He was crashing down the hill.
c.   He was crashing toward the sea.
d.   The frightening laughter was echoing back.

Based on a sentence by Theodore Taylor, *The Cay*

2a.   Finny and I went along the Boardwalk.
b.   We were in our sneakers and white slacks.
c.   Finny was in a light blue polo shirt.
d.   I was in a T-shirt.

Based on a sentence by John Knowles, *A Separate Peace*

3a.   It happened all the time he was reading the newspaper.
b.   What happened was that his wife leaned out of the window.
c.   His wife was a fat woman with a white face.

d. She was gazing into the street.

e. Her thick white arms were folded under her loose breast on the window sill.

Based on a sentence by Bernard Malamud, "A Summer's Reading"

4a. To the right of them the gym meditated.

b. It meditated behind its gray walls.

c. The windows were shining back at the sun.

d. The windows were high.

e. The windows were wide.

f. The windows were oval-topped.

Based on a sentence by John Knowles, *A Separate Peace*

PRACTICING THE SKILL: SENTENCE EXPANDING

In this part (unlike in the previous parts on sentence scrambling, sentence imitating, and sentence combining) you have to supply both the structure and *the content* without any help from model sentences. You are doing almost all of the work on your own, unaided by models. Your ability to expand sentences by using absolute phrases can be a strong indicator of how well you can add this skill permanently to your writing style.

In all of the sentence expanding Practices, follow the same guidelines. First, select content that blends well with the content of the author's sentence. Second, express that content through absolute phrases. Punctuate correctly.

PRACTICE 12

Add an absolute phrase to each of the reduced sentences below, blending your content with the rest of the sentence. Each of the sentences (in its original, complete version) had an absolute phrase in the place indicated by the slash mark. When you finish, compare your sentence with the original in the References.

Reduced Sentence

Catherine looked at me all the time, / .

Student-Expanded Sentence

Catherine looked at me all the time, **her concern about the coming storm unspoken**.

Original Sentence by Author

Catherine looked at me all the time, **her eyes happy**.

Ernest Hemingway, *A Farewell to Arms*

Practice a variety of lengths and degrees of modification for your absolute phrases. Don't be disappointed if your content is unlike that of the original. In sentence expanding, you're not trying to imitate. You're trying to imagine both content and structure (absolute phrase) that will work well when blended with the rest of the author's sentence.

1.   He began scrambling up the wooden pegs nailed to the side of the tree, / .

From a sentence by John Knowles, A Separate Peace

2.   They were smiling, / , / . (compound absolute phrases)

From a sentence by Jack Finney, "Of Missing Persons"

3.   Touser roused himself under Fowler's desk and scratched another flea, / .

From a sentence by Clifford D. Simak, "Desertion"

4.   Men, / , / , swung by; a few women all muffled scurried along; and one tiny boy, / , was jerked along angrily between his father and mother; he looked like a baby fly that had fallen into the cream. (compound absolute phrases)

From a sentence by Katherine Mansfield, "The Voyage"

PRACTICE 13

In the last Practice, the length of the absolute phrases you added to the authors' sentences was your choice. Here, try to add approximately the same number of words the authors used for their absolute phrases. The number of words in the original absolute phrase, including modification within the phrase, is indicated next to the slash mark. Most of the absolute phrases in the original sentences are long and highly modified. In the following examples, all from Jack London's *Call of the Wild*, notice how London achieves his highly modified absolute phrases. The main words in the absolute phrase are capitalized; the modifiers are in boldface.

1.   Even Perrault had to grin one morning after that, when Francois forgot to put them on him and Buck lay on his back, **his** FEET WAVING **appealingly in the air**, and refused to budge without them.

2.   When the long winter nights come on, and the wolves follow their meat into the lower valleys, he may be seen running again at the head of the pack through the pale moonlight or glimmering borealis, leaping gigantic above his fellows, **his great** THROAT A-BELLOWING **as he sings a song of the younger world**, which is the song of the pack.

3.   He staggered limply about, **BLOOD** FLOWING **from nose and mouth and ears, his beautiful** COAT SPRAYED **and** FLECKED **with it.** (compound absolute phrases)

Remember, add content that blends smoothly with the rest of the author's sentence, using a highly modified absolute phrase that meets or exceeds the number of words next to the slash mark.

The main words of the absolute phrase from the original sentence are provided to get you started. You provide the modifiers.

1.   His great chest was low to the ground, /5 his **HEAD** ..., /5 his **FEET** ..., /10 the **CLAWS**. ... (compound absolute phrases)

From a sentence by Jack London, *Call of the Wild*

2.   Now, in the waning daylight, he turned into Glover Street toward his home, /10 his **ARMS**. ...

From a sentence by Norman Katkov, "The Torn Invitation"

3.   As they drove off Wilson saw her standing under the big tree, looking pretty rather than beautiful in her faintly rosy khaki, /17 **her dark HAIR** ..., /12 her **FACE**. ... (compound absolute phrases)

From a sentence by Ernest Hemingway, "The Short Happy Life of Francis Macomber"

4.   In front of the house where we lived, the mountain went down steeply to the little plain along the lake, and we sat on the porch of the house in the sun and saw the winding of the road down the mountain-side and the terraced vineyards on the side of the lower mountain, /8 the **VINES** ... **and** /6 the **FIELDS** ..., and below the vineyards, /13 the **HOUSES**. ... (compound absolute phrases)

From a sentence by Ernest Hemingway, *A Farewell to Arms*

3

Sentence Composing
with Appositive Phrases

IDENTIFYING THE SKILL

Here is a list of sentences, all of which were written by professional writers. However, some parts have been deleted.

1.   It went away slowly.
2.   The land that lay stretched out before him became of vast significance.
3.   However, I looked with a mixture of admiration and awe at Peter.
4.   That night in the south upstairs chamber Emmett lay in a kind of trance.

Now compare the above sentences with the originals. Notice that the part deleted, when combined with the reduced sentence above, accounts for the distinctiveness of the author's original sentence.

1a.   It went away slowly, **the feeling of disappointment that came sharply after the thrill that made his shoulders ache**.
                                     Ernest Hemingway, "Big Two-Hearted River: Part II"
2a.   The land that lay stretched out before him became of vast significance, **a place peopled by his fancy with a new race of men sprung from himself**.
                                     Sherwood Anderson, *Winesburg, Ohio*
3a.   However, I looked with a mixture of admiration and awe at Peter, **a boy who could and did imitate a police siren every morning on his way to the showers**.
                                     Robert Russell, *To Catch an Angel*
4a.   That night in the south upstairs chamber, **a hot little room where a full-leafed chinaberry tree shut all the air from the single window**, Emmett lay in a kind of trance.
                                     Jessamyn West, "A Time of Learning"

40

The boldface phrases are appositives, another of the sentence parts that differentiate professional writing from student writing. They are frequently used in professional writing but rarely appear in student writing. Appositive phrases are an efficient way to combine related ideas in one sentence.

CHARACTERISTICS OF APPOSITIVE PHRASES

Definition

An appositive is a noun or (much less often) a pronoun that identifies an adjacent noun or pronoun. An appositive phrase is the appositive word plus any of its modifiers. Here are examples. The complete appositive phrase is in boldface.

1.   Poppa, **a good quiet man**, spent the last hours before our parting moving aimlessly about the yard, keeping to himself and avoiding me.
Gordon Parks, "My Mother's Dream for Me"

2.   The boy looked at them, **big black ugly insects**.
Doris Lessing, *African Stories*

3.   Hour after hour he stood there, silent, motionless, **a shadow carved in ebony and moonlight**.
James V. Marshall, *Walkabout*

4.   A man, **a weary old pensioner with a bald dirty head and a stained brown corduroy waistcoat**, appeared at the door of a small gate lodge.
Brian Moore, *The Lonely Passion of Judith Hearne*

5.   He had the appearance of a man who had done a great thing, **something greater than any ordinary man would do**.
John Henrik Clarke, "The Boy Who Painted Christ Black"

Position

An appositive phrase can be used as a sentence opener (preceding a clause), as an S-V split (splitting the subject and verb of a clause), or as a sentence closer (following a clause).

Punctuation

When the appositive phrase is a sentence opener (introductory position), a comma follows it.

One of eleven brothers and sisters, Harriet was a moody, willful child.
Langston Hughes, "Road to Freedom"

When the appositive phrase is an S-V split (intermediate position), commas precede and follow it.

Van'ka Zhukov, **a boy of nine who had been apprenticed to the shoemaker Alyakhin three months ago,** was staying up that Christmas Eve.

Anton Chekhov, "Van'ka"

When the appositive phrase is a sentence closer (terminal position), a comma precedes the phrase and a period follows it.

At once Fujiko got up and motioned him to wait as she rushed noiselessly for the swords that lay in front of the takonama, **the little alcove of honor.**

James Clavell, *Shogun*

PRACTICE 1

Each of the professionally written sentences below contains an appositive phrase. For each sentence, do the following:

(a)   Identify the appositive phrase, the appositive word, and its modifiers.

(b)   Name the word(s) that the appositive phrase identifies.

(c)   State the position of the appositive phrase (sentence opener, S-V split, sentence closer).

(d)   Punctuate the appositive phrase correctly.

1.   The face of Liliana Methold the fifth woman in the plane was badly bruised and covered with blood.

Piers Paul Read, *Alive*

2.   One of these dogs the best one had disappeared.

Fred Gipson, *Old Yeller*

3.   Mr. Mick Malloy cashier at the Ulster and Connaught Bank draped his grey sports jacket neatly on a hanger and put on his black shantung work coat.

Brian Moore, *The Lonely Passion of Judith Hearne*

4.   A self-educated man he had accepted the necessary smattering facts of science with a serene indulgence, as simply so much further proof of what the Creator could do when He put His hand to it.

Wilbur Daniel Steele, "The Man Who Saw through Heaven"

5.   Halfway there he heard the sound he dreaded the hollow, rasping cough of a horse.

John Steinbeck, *The Red Pony*

6.   The writer an old man with a white mustache had some difficulty in getting into bed.

Sherwood Anderson, *Winesburg, Ohio*

7.   In our clenched fists we held our working cards from the shop those sacred cards that we thought meant security.

Gerda Weissmann Klein, *All But My Life*

PRACTICING THE SKILL: SENTENCE SCRAMBLING

Practice flexibility in the positioning of appositive phrases in the sentences you compose. An appositive phrase may occur in any of three positions.

Sentence Opener (Introductory)

One of eleven brothers and sisters, Harriet was a moody, willful child.

S-V Split (Intermediate)

Harriet, **one of eleven brothers and sisters**, was a moody, willful child.

Sentence Closer (Terminal)

Harriet was a moody, willful child, **one of eleven brothers and sisters**.

Sometimes the positions are interchangeable, as in the above three positionings of the appositive phrase. Which of the three to use will depend on such things as sentence variety, the relative emphasis desired, and the relationship between the structure and content of the sentence and the other sentences in the paragraph.

Sometimes only two of the three positions are options; the third would result in unacceptable grammar, poor modification, or lack of emphasis. In the repositionings below, the terminal position is inferior to the introductory or intermediate positions.

Introductory

A boy of nine who had been apprenticed to the shoemaker Alyakhin three months ago, Van'ka Zhukov was staying up that Christmas Eve.

Intermediate

Van'ka Zhukov, **a boy of nine who had been apprenticed to the shoemaker Alyakhin three months ago**, was staying up that Christmas Eve.

Terminal (Unacceptable)

Van'ka Zhukov was staying up that Christmas Eve, **a boy of nine who had been apprenticed to the shoemaker Alyakhin three months ago**.

Sometimes only one of the three positions may be acceptable grammatically. In the repositionings below, only the terminal position is acceptable:

Introductory (Unacceptable)

Big black ugly insects, the boy looked at them.

Intermediate (Unacceptable)

The boy, **big black ugly insects,** looked at them.

Terminal

The boy looked at them, **big black ugly insects.**

PRACTICE 2

Unscramble each list of sentence parts three times: first to produce a sentence with the appositive phrase in the introductory position; next, in the intermediate position; and finally, in the terminal position. Classify the use of each position as either acceptable or unacceptable. If two (or all three) positions are acceptable, indicate which you prefer and why. Punctuate correctly.

1a. her blonde hair flowing down her back
 b. a fragile-faced beauty not yet ten years old
 c. sat demurely
 d. she
2a. hung up her spurs
 b. tired from the long ride
 c. a twelve-year-old daredevil rider
 d. Rosemary
3a. at the ineptitude of her competitors
 b. Nadia
 c. the star gymnast who captured the world with her performance
 d. smiled softly
4a. the king of rock and roll and the subject of controversy
 b. left behind
 c. Elvis Presley
 d. millions of bereaved fans

Sentences may contain more than one appositive phrase. If the multiple appositive phrases identify the same noun or pronoun, they are called "compound." If the multiple appositive phrases identify different nouns or pronouns, they are each called "simple."

Examples of Multiple Appositive Phrases

Compound

The sound of the approaching grain teams was louder, **THUD of big hooves on hard ground, DRAG of brakes,** and **the JINGLE of trace chains.**

John Steinbeck, *Of Mice and Men*

Here the three appositive words identify the same noun: *sound.*

Simple

Once Enoch Bentley, **the older ONE of the boys,** struck his father, **old TOM BENTLEY,** with the butt of a teamster's whip, and the old man seemed likely to die.

Sherwood Anderson, Winesburg, Ohio

Here one of the appositive words identifies one noun (*Enoch Bentley*); the other appositive word identifies a different noun (*father*).

PRACTICE 3

Each of the scrambled sentences below contains multiple appositive phrases, either compound or simple. Unscramble each sentence to produce the most effective arrangement of the sentence parts. Punctuate correctly. For sentences with compound appositive phrases, you must decide the best order in which to arrange them. When you finish, compare your sentence with the original in the References. How does yours differ? Which do you like better? Why?

1a. talked continually of virginity
  b. the son of a jeweler in Winesburg
  c. one of them
  d. a slender young man with white hands

From a sentence by Sherwood Anderson, Winesburg, Ohio

2a. went over to Tom Willy's saloon
  b. in the late afternoon
  c. Will Henderson
  d. and editor of the *Eagle*
  e. owner

From a sentence by Sherwood Anderson, Winesburg, Ohio

3a. who had made his kill
  b. Buck stood and looked on
  c. the dominant primordial beast
  d. and found it good
  e. the successful champion

From a sentence by Jack London, Call of the Wild

4a. with devil-may-care eyes and a long humorous nose
  b. with a dignified face
  c. Mr. Mick Malloy
  d. tall cashier
  e. a nice sort of fellow

f.   tall, young secret gambler

g.   a gentlemanly bank clerk

h.   became Mr. Malloy
     From a sentence by Brian Moore, *The Lonely Passion of Judith Hearne*

5a. books

b.   through the window

c.   everything necessary

d.   wine

e.   by sending a note

f.   he could receive

g.   music

h.   in any quantity
     From a sentence by Anton Chekhov, "The Bet"

PRACTICING THE SKILL: SENTENCE IMITATING

Here is an exceptionally long sentence, one containing compound appositive phrases in a series. The sentence is taken from *The Martian Chronicles* by Ray Bradbury. It is one sentence from a two-sentence chapter, "The Old Ones." The short chapter describes the coming of elderly people to Mars. Each sentence is a separate paragraph. Here is the chapter:

"The Old Ones"

And what more natural than that, at last, the old people come to Mars, following in the trail left by the loud frontiersmen, the aromatic sophisticates, and the professional travelers and romantic lecturers in search of new grist.

And so the dry and crackling people, the people who spent their time listening to their hearts and feeling their pulses and spooning syrups into their wry mouths, these people who once had taken chair cars to California in November and third-class steamers to Italy in April, the dried-apricot people, the mummy people, came at last to Mars.

The second sentence consists mainly of highly modified compound appositive phrases. If we removed all of them, what remains would be the main clause:

And so the dry and crackling people came at last to Mars.

The compound appositive phrases are all in the intermediate position (between the subject *people* and its verb *came*). Compare the following sentence with the one by Bradbury:

And then the unemployed and desperate actors, the actors who filled their days yearning for parts and badgering their agents and pounding the pavements for some lucky audition, these actors who had wanted stage careers on

Broadway since infancy and movie careers in Hollywood since birth, the bright-lights actors, the moth actors, arrived in droves at the casting office.

This sentence is an imitation of the structure of Bradbury's sentence. Like Bradbury's, it contains highly modified compound appositive phrases in the intermediate position.

PRACTICE 4

Underneath the model sentence are three imitations. Both the model and the imitations contain appositive phrases. The imitations are presented as a list of scrambled sentence parts for you to unscramble to duplicate the structure of the model. The first imitation uses nonsense language to help you focus on structural similarities between the scrambled sentence and the model. The two other imitations use sense language. Unscramble each of the three sentences to produce a sentence similar in structure to the model. In addition, identify the sentence part in the scrambled list that is the appositive phrase and tell what noun (or pronoun) it identifies.

Model

Beside the fireplace old Doctor Winter sat, bearded and simple and benign, **historian and physician to the town.**

John Steinbeck, The Moon Is Down

Scrambled Nonsense Imitation

1a. froopy and pasty and tumeous
 b. the big stonnert ladled
 c. the blurt and the temician of the beach
 d. near the croop

Scrambled Sense Imitation

2a. president and valedictorian of the senior class
 b. by the podium
 c. intelligent and composed and smiling
 d. scholarly Henrietta stood

Scrambled Sense Imitation

3a. beaming and affectionate and happy
 b. the bride and groom in their finery
 c. they danced
 d. under the canopy

PRACTICE 5

The model sentence here is broken into the four sentence parts that you unscrambled, arranged in the same order in which they occur in the model. For each part from the model, list the equivalent part from each of the scrambled versions. After providing the equivalent sentence parts, write two of your own sentences imitating the model, one sentence part at a time.

First Sentence Part

Model: Beside the fireplace

Second Sentence Part

Model: old Doctor Winter sat,

Third Sentence Part

Model: bearded and simple and benign,

Fourth Sentence Part (Appositive Phrase)

Model: historian and physician to the town.

PRACTICE 6

This Practice will review appositive phrases as well as provide examples of imitations of models. Later Practices, in which you do the imitating, will be easier for having done this exercise.

First, read the model sentence carefully, paying special attention to the structure: position, type, and number of sentence parts; punctuation; and so forth. Next, read through the three sentences underneath the model and, again paying special attention to the parts of each of the three sentences, identify the one sentence that is an imitation of the model.

This Practice contains nonsense language, which will make it easier for you to focus primarily on the *way* and not the *what* of the sentence: the structure, not the content.

In each model the appositive phrase is in boldface.

1.   *Model:* She stied as usual to creestan her merted, solorious, greendly pearing, **a kind of yoost all over her remption.**
A.   When upshuded, when berooded, straining near the shopmert, he cransted over fifty blams to deliver no more than two plops.
B.   Frank bleeped so hard to mulch the blomed, weet, varnly quickette, a type of frinch way down the wump.

C. Glooster wangled nearing the fraport, his flathe cowering in tangerines, studying twenty tulips of light darkness.

2. *Model:* **One of many green moops of sun circles**, each circle dancing in marched zits, the tiny circle trod the long path in the hot winter cloud.
A. When they danced away the mileage, crested for the pordid, scringling warmps, Sally asked the toogler its belhound.
B. There, crusted with mellows, a zigote blamed the covering potsherd, its beak stuck in the simples by sunlight.
C. First of some bleeded turnips with apples, each one fresting with two pits, this one bounded a wall near the two green pillows.

3. *Model:* The Ming, **an old, three-legged crast in a soft stone sweater**, had stopped blurping the loons and was stavering with some hambers he had beaten with the top of a greasy grass.
A. Its penals rezorming its blath and blandid seets, the mazer became weekly less seamy in sterning it with cacots, in corving its madles, which were always corned and muffled in tables.
B. Mr. Mister, the flown, great-berried wush with the fried zezzled meeskite, was beginning sturching the hounds and was binioning near many steaks he had hatched in the fourth carton of fresh ashtrays.
C. Near the wallow in the hollow of the blank beederds, because the stream had teetered in depthly tones that sarborded twenty of the frandoles, a long, sleek zender coorsed twenty cups, stewing them.

If you were able to pick out the imitation of the model, you saw that structure, like content, is something you can *read*. Noticing structure, both in the sentences of professional writers and in your own, is an important skill to develop—one that will help you write mature sentences easily.

PRACTICE 7

Now that you are familiar with the structure of the model sentences from the previous Practice, your work here will be simple. In this Practice, write two sentence imitations for each of the three models in the previous Practice, using their sentence structure but providing your own content.

Each sentence below is the original of the nonsense models in the last Practice. First, tell which sentence matches which model. Then, write two imitations: a nonsense imitation and a sense imitation. The appositive phrases are in boldface.

1. She struggled as usual to maintain her calm, composed, friendly bearing, **a sort of mask she wore all over her body**.
D. H. Lawrence, "The Blind Man"

2.   The judge, **an old, bowlegged fellow in a pale-blue sweater,** had stopped examining the animals and was reading over some notes he had taken on the back of a dirty envelope.

Jessamyn West, "The Lesson"

3.   **One of many small groups of children,** each child carrying his little bag of crackling, we trod the long road home in the cold winter afternoon.

Peter Abrahams, *Tell Freedom*

PRACTICE 8

In this last Practice on sentence imitating using appositive phrases, you can test your ability to imitate model sentences without any aid other than the model.

The model sentences are arranged in four groups according to the position of the appositive phrase. Imitating the structure of the model sentence, but using your own content, write a sentence for each of the models below. Imitate the structure of the entire sentence, not just the appositive phrase.

Introductory Appositive Phrases (Sentence Openers)

1.   **One of eleven brothers and sisters,** Harriet was a moody, willful child.

Langston Hughes, "Road to Freedom"

2.   **A self-educated man,** he had accepted the necessary smattering facts of science with a serene indulgence, as simply so much further proof of what the Creator could do when He put His Hand to it.

Wilbur Daniel Steele, "The Man Who Saw through Heaven"

Intermediate Appositive Phrases (S-V Splits)

3.   One of these, **a young woman who turned to look,** called to Yakov, but by then the wagon was out of the marketplace, scattering some chickens nesting in the ruts of the road and a flock of jabbering ducks, as it clattered on.

Bernard Malamud, *The Fixer*

4.   They cannot possibly know that they, **ex-slave and ex-master,** cannot be used as their fathers were used—that all identities, in short, are in question, are about to be made new.

James Baldwin, "Every Good-bye Ain't Gone"

5.   Henry Strader, **an old man who had been on the farm since Jesse came into possession and who before David's time had never been known to make a joke,** made the same joke every morning.

Sherwood Anderson, *Winesburg, Ohio*

Terminal Appositive Phrases (Sentence Closers)

6.   In all the years which have since elapsed, she remains the woman I loved and lost, **the unattainable one.**

Henry Miller, *Stand Still Like a Hummingbird*

7.   It had a black spot on it, **the black spot Mr. Summer had made the night before with the heavy pencil in the coal-company office.**

Shirley Jackson, "The Lottery"

8.   The warmth of the rays drew this opaqueness up into little spirals of mist, **random smoke rings from a giant's pipe that floated lazily over the billabong.**

James V. Marshall, *Walkabout*

Multiple Positions

9.   After a word with the lieutenant, he went a few paces higher, and sat there, **a dominant figure,** his sweat-marked horse swishing its tail, while he looked down on his men, on his orderly, **a nonentity among the crowd.**

D. H. Lawrence, "The Prussian Officer"

10.   Mr. Mick Malloy, **tall, young secret gambler with devil-may-care eyes and a long humorous nose,** became Mr. Malloy, **tall cashier with a dignified face, a gentlemanly bank clerk, a nice sort of fellow.**

Brian Moore, *The Lonely Passion of Judith Hearne*

PRACTICING THE SKILL: SENTENCE COMBINING

In this part you'll produce single sentences from lists derived from sentences by professional writers. Each of the original sentences contains an appositive phrase. In the References are the originals for you to compare with yours. In sentence combining you have to make more choices about sentence structure than you did in sentence imitating. In sentence combining, you must decide what form or structure to give a list of sentences as you combine them into just one sentence.

PRACTICE 9

In one of the sentences in each group, a slash mark (/) indicates that the original sentence has an appositive phrase at that place. Combine the sentences underneath into an appositive phrase that will fit smoothly into the place. Write an imitation of the resulting sentence, using your own content and the structure of the model. For example:

Sentence One: She was playing the Canteen at Aldershot at the time, / .
Sentence Two: The theatre was grubby.
Sentence Three: The theatre was mean.
Sentence Four: The theatre was catering mostly to soldiers.

Combination with Appositive Phrase

She was playing the Canteen at Aldershot at the time, **a grubby, mean theatre catering mostly to soldiers.**

Charles Spencer Chaplin (Charlie Chaplin), *My Autobiography*

Imitation

He was inspecting a condemned school near Thorn Road around noon, **an old, stone building closing probably in June**.

1a. On this Sunday morning the postman and the policeman had gone fishing in the boat of Mr. Corell, / .

b. Mr. Corell was the store-keeper.

c. He was popular.

Based on a sentence by John Steinbeck, *The Moon Is Down*

2a. The real estate agent, / , soon joined them.

b. The agent was a man.

c. He was old.

d. He had a face.

e. The face was smiling.

f. The face was hypocritical.

Based on a sentence by Willa Cather, "The Sculptor's Funeral"

3a. They approached the domed synagogue with its iron weathercock, / , for the time being resting in peace.

b. The synagogue was a yellow-walled building.

c. It was pock-marked.

d. It had a door.

e. The door was oak.

Based on a sentence by Bernard Malamud, *The Fixer*

4a. Lieutenant Tonder was a poet, / .

b. He was a bitter poet.

c. He was a poet who dreamed of perfect, ideal love.

d. The love was of elevated young men for girls.

e. The girls were poor.

Based on a sentence by John Steinbeck, *The Moon Is Down*

5a. Out of the flaming wreckage was born another of the legends surrounding the Stanley Steamer, / .

b. The Stanley Steamer was the best car of its era.

c. However, also the Stanley Steamer was the most misunderstood.

d. In addition, it was the most maligned.

Based on a sentence by John Carlova, *American Heritage*

PRACTICE 10

Below you are given a model sentence and then a list of sentences to be combined to resemble the structure of the model. In addition to practicing the use of appositive phrases, you will practice other sentence composing skills used by the authors of the model sentences. You may not know the names of the other skills, but you will be able to imitate them if you follow the directions for this Practice. The names aren't important; your use of the skills is.

First, read the model several times, paying special attention to the structure of the sentence. In each model the appositive phrase is in boldface. Study it. Also, study the rest of the sentence carefully; you'll need to be familiar with not only the appositive phrase but also the rest of the sentence structure.

Next, read the list of sentences underneath the model. Combine these into one sentence having basically the same structure as the model. The order in which the sentences are listed is the order of the parts of the model. In other words, convert the first sentence into the first sentence part of the model, the second sentence into the second part, and so forth.

Finally, write an imitation of the model, keeping the same structure but providing your own content. For example:

Model

Mr. Cattanzara, **a stocky, bald-headed man who worked in a change booth on an IRT station,** lived on the next block after George's, above a shoe repair store.

Bernard Malamud, "A Summer's Reading"

Sentences to Be Converted	*Conversions*
1. This is about Jan Carter.	1. Jan Carter,
2. She is an unabashed, sun-tanned flirt.	2. an unabashed, sun-tanned flirt
3. She had smiled at him in the cafeteria line.	3. who had smiled at him in the cafeteria line,
4. She transferred to the department near Tom's.	4. transferred to the department near Tom's,
5. She transferred for a "chance" meeting.	5. for a "chance" meeting.

Imitation

Tom Zengler, the slower, more heavy-handed pianist who had studied under Professor Samione for a decade, performed in the recital hall near Jacob's, with an obvious competitive attitude.

Here are the three sentences with their equivalent sentence parts.

Model	*Combination*	*Imitation*
1. Mr. Cattanzara,	1. Jan Carter,	1. Tom Zengler,
2. a stocky, bald-headed man	2. an unabashed, sun-tanned flirt	2. the slower, more heavy-handed pianist

3. who worked in a
change booth on an
IRT station,

3. who had smiled at him
in the cafeteria line,

3. who had studied
under Professor Samione for a decade,

4. lived on the next
block after George's,

4. transferred to the department near Tom's,

4. performed in the
recital hall near
Jacob's,

5. above a shoe repair
store.

5. for a "chance" meeting.

5. with an obvious
competitive attitude.

Here are the three sentences from this example: same structure, different content. Appositive phrases are in boldface.

Model

Mr. Cattanzara, **a stocky, bald-headed man who worked in a change booth on an IRT station**, lived on the next block after George's, above a shoe repair store.

Combination

Jan Carter, **an unabashed, sun-tanned flirt who had smiled at him in the cafeteria line**, transferred to the department near Tom's, for a "chance" meeting.

Imitation

Tom Zengler, **the slower, more heavy-handed pianist who had studied under Professor Samione for a decade**, performed in the recital hall near Jacob's, with an obvious competitive attitude.

Convert one sentence at a time into a structure resembling the equivalent sentence part of the model sentence. Continue until you have converted all the sentences into such structures.

A. *Model:* Among the company was a lawyer, **a young man of about twenty-five**.

Anton Chekhov, "The Bet"

1. She was near the statue.
2. She was an obvious tourist.
3. She was an oriental lady.
4. She had a Kodak camera.

B. *Model:* Sady Ellison, **the daughter of Long Butt Ellison**, worked as a waitress for Turkey Plott in a defiant and condescending fashion.

Wayne Kernodle, "Last of the Rugged Individualists"

1. This is about *Gone with the Wind*.
2. That is the movie with the most re-issues.
3. It originated as a novel.
4. The novel was of the old South.
5. The novel was by someone who was un-glamorous.
6. The someone was also unknown.
7. The someone was an authoress.

C.   *Model:* Captain Bentick was a family man, **a lover of dogs and pink children and Christmas**.

John Steinbeck, *The Moon Is Down*

1. "Missouri" is a casserole.
2. The casserole is special.
3. It is a blend.
4. It has potatoes.
5. It has tomatoes.
6. The tomatoes are stewed.
7. It has hamburger.

D.   *Model:* He was close to twenty and had needs with the neighborhood girls, but no money to spend, and he couldn't get more than an occasional few cents because his father was poor, and his sister Sophie, who resembled George, **a tall, bony girl of twenty-three**, earned very little, and what she had she kept for herself.

Bernard Malamud, "A Summer's Reading"

1. We were far from our destination.
2. In addition, we were making good time on the interstate.
3. But there was no time to squander.
4. In addition, Dad wouldn't stop more than twice a day.
5. Although we kids were itchy, he wouldn't stop.
6. In addition, Mom was the one who kept the peace.
7. She was a shrewd, gentle arbitrator.
8. She had Solomon's mind.
9. She circumvented some flare-ups.
10. And she did something with those she couldn't circumvent.
11. She left those to Heaven.

PRACTICE 11

Combine each list of sentences into one sentence containing an appositive phrase. Underline each phrase. You may eliminate words and change their form as long as the intended meaning remains. Punctuate correctly. When you finish, compare your work with the original sentences in the References.

1a. Something happens at the gate.

   b. There, I show the pass to a private.

   c. The private is young.

   d. The private is Japanese.

   e. The private is the sentry.

                                                Based on a sentence by Richard E. Kim, *Lost Names*

2a. It happened when he was twelve.

   b. Then, his mother married an executive.

   c. The executive was of a machine tool company.

   d. The company was in Cleveland.

   e. The executive was an engineer.

   f. He was an engineer who had adult children of his own.

                        Based on a sentence by Glendon Swarthout, *Bless the Beasts and Children*

3a. My patient was a woman.

   b. She was modern.

   c. She was intelligent.

   d. She with her five children seemed trapped.

   e. She seemed as trapped as her forebears.

   f. Her forebears were in Victorian times.

   g. In Victorian times was before the emancipation of women.

                                Based on a sentence by Rollo May, *Love and Will*

4a. On the bark of the tree was scored something.

   b. What was scored there was a name.

   c. The name was of Deacon Peabody.

   d. Deacon Peabody was a man.

   e. He was eminent.

   f. It was he who had waxed wealthy.

   g. He did this by driving bargains.

   h. The bargains were shrewd.

   i. The bargains were with the Indians.

                    Based on a sentence by Washington Irving, "The Devil and Tom Walker"

PRACTICING THE SKILL: SENTENCE EXPANDING

In this part (unlike in the previous parts on sentence scrambling, sentence imitating, and sentence combining) you have to supply both the structure and *the content* without any help from model sentences. You are doing almost all of the work on your own, unaided by models. Your ability to expand sentences by using appositive phrases can be a strong indicator of how well you can add this skill permanently to your writing style.

In all of the sentence expanding Practices, follow the same guidelines. First, select content that blends well with the content of the author's sentence. Second, express that content through appositive phrases. Punctuate correctly.

PRACTICE 12

Add an appositive phrase to each of the reduced sentences below, blending your content with the rest of the sentence. Each of the sentences (in its original, complete version) had an appositive phrase in the place indicated by the slash mark. When you finish, compare your sentence with the original in the References.

Reduced Sentence

At the controls was Mike Forney, / .

Student-Expanded Sentence

At the controls was Mike Forney, **a shrewd but well-liked foreman with allegiances equally shared between his men and his boss.**

Original Sentence by Author

At the controls was Mike Forney, **a tough twenty-seven year old from Chicago.**

James Michener, *The Bridges at Toko-Ri*

Practice a variety of lengths and degrees of modification for your appositive phrases. Don't be disappointed if your content is unlike that of the original. In sentence expanding, you're not trying to imitate. You're trying to imagine both content and structure (appositive phrase) that will work well when blended with the rest of the author's sentence.

1. He, / , had fled because of his superior perceptions and knowledge.
   From a sentence by Stephen Crane, *The Red Badge of Courage*

2. There was Major Hunter, / , / . (compound appositive phrases)
   From a sentence by John Steinbeck, *The Moon Is Down*

3. My bed was an army cot, / .
   From a sentence by James Thurber, "The Night the Bed Fell"

4. I had hardly any patience with the serious work of life which, not that it stood between me and desire, seemed to me child's play, / .
   From a sentence by James Joyce, "Araby"

PRACTICE 13

In the last Practice, the length of the appositive phrases you added to the authors' sentences was your choice. Here, try to add approximately the same
number of words that the authors used for their appositive phrases. The number of words in the original appositive phrase, including modification within
the phrase, is indicated next to the slash mark. Most of the appositive phrases
in the original sentences are long and highly modified, with modification occurring both before and after the appositive word (noun or pronoun) within
the appositive phrase. In the following examples, notice how the author
achieves a highly modified appositive phrase by placing modifiers both before
and after the appositive word. The appositive word is capitalized; the modifiers are in boldface. Notice that most of the modification occurs after the appositive word.

1.   That night in the south upstairs chamber, **a hot little ROOM where a
full-leafed chinaberry tree shut all the air from the single window**, Emmett
lay in a kind of trance.
                                        Jessamyn West, "A Time of Learning"

2.   The fifth traveler, **a withered old GENTLEMAN sitting next to the
middle door across the aisle**, napped fitfully upon his cane.
                                        Henry Sydnor Harrison, "Miss Hinch"

3.   The sound of the approaching grain teams was louder, **THUD of big
hooves on hard ground**, **DRAG of brakes**, and **the JINGLE of trace chains**.
(compound appositive phrases)
                                        John Steinbeck, *Of Mice and Men*

4.   Henry Strader, **an old MAN who had been on the farm since Jesse
came into possession and who before David's time had never been known to
make a joke**, made the same joke every morning.
                                        Sherwood Anderson, *Winesburg, Ohio*

Remember, add content that blends smoothly with the rest of the author's
sentence, using a highly modified appositive phrase that meets or exceeds the
number of words next to the slash mark.

The appositive word from the original sentence is provided to get you
started. You provide its modifiers.

1.   Perhaps two or three times a year we would come together at a party,
one of those teen-age affairs which last until dawn with singing and dancing
and silly games such as "Kiss the Pillow," or "Post Office," **/21 the GAME
which** . . . .
                          From a sentence by Henry Miller, *Stand Still Like a Hummingbird*

2.   Thus, one noontime, coming back from the office lunch downstairs a
little earlier than usual, he found her and several of the foreign-family girls, as

well as four of the American girls, surrounding Polish Mary, /**11 ONE of the** ..., who was explaining in rather a high key how a certain "feller" whom she had met the night before had given her a beaded bag, and for what purpose.

From a sentence by Theodore Dreiser, *An American Tragedy*

3.   The rest were standing around in hatless, smoky little groups of twos and threes and fours inside the heated waiting room, talking in voices that, almost without exception, sounded collegiately dogmatic, as though each young man, in his strident, conversational turn, was clearing up, once and for all, some highly controversial issue, /**14 ONE that** ....

From a sentence by J. D. Salinger, *Franny and Zooey*

4.   Out in the distances the fans of windmills twinkled, turning, and about the base of each, about the drink tank, was a speckle of dark dots, /**17 a GATHER of cattle** ....

From a sentence by Glendon Swarthout, *Bless the Beasts and Children*

4

Sentence Composing with Participle Phrases

IDENTIFYING THE SKILL

Here is a list of sentences, all of which were written by professional writers. However, some parts have been deleted.

1. Spencer took half an hour.
2. But Sadao had his reward.
3. The sun rose clear and bright.
4. He sat on a bench here.
5. We could see the lake and the mountains across the lake on the French side.
6. Adolph Knipe took a sip of stout.

Now compare the above sentences with the originals. Notice that the part deleted, when combined with the reduced sentence above, accounts for the distinctiveness of the author's original sentence.

1a. Spencer took half an hour, **swimming in one of the pools which was filled with the seasonal rain, waiting for the pursuers to catch up to him.**
Ray Bradbury, *The Martian Chronicles*

2a. But Sadao, **searching the spot of black in the twilight sea that night,** had his reward.
Pearl S. Buck, "The Enemy"

3a. The sun rose clear and bright, **tinging the foamy crests of the waves with a reddish purple.**
Alexander Dumas, *Count of Monte Cristo*

4a. He sat on a bench here, **watching the leafy trees and the flowers blooming on the inside of the railing, thinking of a better life for himself.**
Bernard Malamud, "A Summer's Reading"

60

5a. **Sitting up in bed eating breakfast,** we could see the lake and the mountains across the lake on the French side.

Ernest Hemingway, A Farewell to Arms

6a. Adolph Knipe took a sip of stout, **tasting the malty-bitter flavor, feeling the trickle of cold liquid as it traveled down his throat and settled in the top of his stomach, cool at first, then spreading and becoming warm, making a little area of warmness inside of him.**

Roald Dahl, "The Great Automatic Grammatisator"

The boldface phrases are participles, one of the sentence parts that differentiate professional writing from student writing. They are frequently used in professional writing, but rarely appear in student writing. Participle phrases are an efficient way to combine related ideas into one sentence.

In the preceding sections of this book, you studied two other structures (absolute phrases and appositive phrases) that are used frequently by professionals and infrequently by students. Even though those two structures are quite common in professional writing, this one (participle phrases) is the most common, occurring so frequently that you can find examples on almost any page of a book.

CHARACTERISTICS OF PARTICIPLE PHRASES

Definition

A participle phrase is a modifier of a noun or pronoun. The first word in the participle phrase is almost always the participle itself. There are two types of participles. Those called present participles always end in *ing*. Those called past participles almost always end in either *ed* or *en*. Below are examples of both, with the complete participle phrases in boldface, and the noun (or pronoun) modified by the phrase underlined. The participle is capitalized.

Present Participles

1. She was quite far from the windows which were to her left, and behind her were a couple of tall <u>bookcases,</u> **CONTAINING all the books of the factory library**.

John Hersey, Hiroshima

2. Minute <u>fungi</u> overspread the whole exterior, **HANGING in a fine tangled web-work from the eaves**.

Edgar Allan Poe, "The Fall of the House of Usher"

3. **STANDING there in the middle of the street,** <u>Marty</u> suddenly thought of Halloween, of the winter and snowballs, of the schoolyard.

Murray Heyert, "The New Kid"

4. <u>Professor Kazan,</u> **WEARING a spotlessly white tropical suit and a wide-brimmed hat,** was the first ashore.

Arthur C. Clarke, Dolphin Island

5. <u>He</u> walked to the corner of the lot, then back again, **STUDYING the simple terrain as if deciding how best to effect an entry, FROWNING and SCRATCHING his head.** (contains three participles)

Harper Lee, To Kill a Mockingbird

Past Participles

6. In six months a dozen small <u>towns</u> had been laid down upon the naked planet, **FILLED with sizzling neon tubes and yellow electric bulbs.**

Ray Bradbury, The Martian Chronicles

7. The <u>tent,</u> **ILLUMINED by a candle,** glowed warmly in the midst of the white plain.

Jack London, The Call of the Wild

8. **ENCHANTED and ENTHRALLED,** <u>I</u> stopped her constantly for details.

Richard Wright, Black Boy

9. The other shoji slammed open, and **UNSEEN,** <u>Buntaro</u> stamped away, **FOLLOWED by the guard.**

James Clavell, Shogun

10. Her <u>hair,</u> **BRAIDED and WRAPPED around her head,** made an ash-blonde crown.

John Steinbeck, The Grapes of Wrath

Since participle phrases are like partial sentences, you can apply a simple test to identify them. Take the participle phrase and join it to the noun (or pronoun) it modifies with the word *was* (or, for plural nouns, *were*). If the result is a complete sentence, you have correctly identified the participle phrase. For example:

The old <u>man</u> seated himself laboriously, and reached out, **groaning at the movement**, to put another block of peat on the fire.

Walter Van Tilburg Clark, "The Portable Phonograph"

Test for Correct Identification of Participle Phrases

Noun modified	*plus*	was *or* were	*plus*	phrase	*equals*	a sentence.

Sentence:	Man	was	groaning at the movement.

Reread the ten sentences at the beginning of this section of the book. To identify correctly the participle phrases they contain, you can convert each phrase into a sentence. The first five are done for you. Do the rest.

1. Bookcases were containing all the books of the factory library.

2. Fungi were hanging in a fine tangled web-work from the eaves.

3. Marty was standing there in the middle of the street.

4. Kazan was wearing a spotlessly white tropical suit and a wide-brimmed hat.

5. *(three sentences, one for each of the three participle phrases)*
    He was studying the simple terrain as if deciding how best to effect an entry.
    He was frowning.
    He was scratching his head.

This simple test will give you the confidence of knowing you have correctly identified a participle phrase.

Position

A participle phrase can be used as a sentence opener (precedes a clause), S-V split (splits the subject and verb of a clause), or sentence closer (follows a clause).

Sentence Openers (Introductory Position)

1. **Whistling,** he let the escalator waft him into the still night air.
    Ray Bradbury, *Fahrenheit 451*

2. **Looking over their own troops,** they saw mixed masses slowly getting into regular form.
    Stephen Crane, *The Red Badge of Courage*

3. **Amazed at the simplicity of it all,** I understood everything as never before.
    Alphonse Daudet, "The Last Lesson"

4. **Having so much time on his hands,** George thought of going to summer school, but the kids in his classes would be too young.
    Bernard Malamud, "A Summer's Reading"

S-V Splits (Intermediate Position)

5. My father, **cautioning me not to work a horse till he had fed fully,** said I had plenty of time to eat myself.
    Lincoln Steffens, "A Boy on Horseback"

6. Eckels, **balanced on the narrow path,** aimed his rifle playfully.
    Ray Bradbury, "A Sound of Thunder"

7. The sight of Mick's exploring beam of light, **flashing and flickering through the submarine darkness a few yards away,** reminded him that he was not alone.
    Arthur C. Clarke, *Dolphin Island*

8. She climbed into her khakis, **chattering to her mother about the work she was doing,** and hurried to get her horse and be out on the dirt roads for the country air and the radiant green fields of the spring.
    William Allen White, "Mary White"

(*Note:* This sentence contains a participle phrase that splits the second verb from its subject.)

Sentence Closers (Terminal Position)

9. The entire crowd in the saloon gathered about me now, **urging me to drink**.

Richard Wright, *Black Boy*

10. She called to him, **excited**.

Daphne du Maurier, "The Birds"

11. The magician patted the hand, **holding it quietly with a thumb on its blue veins, waiting for life to revive**.

T. S. White, *Book of Merlyn*

12. Laurence nodded again, **indicating that he understood**, but sorrow washed up in his face like a high tide.

Irwin Shaw, "Strawberry Ice Cream Soda"

Note: Terminal position indicates the slot following any S-V group (clause); in this sentence there are two S-V groups, with the participle phrase filling the terminal position after the first S-V group.

Punctuation

When the participle phrase is a sentence opener (introductory position), a comma follows it. When the participle phrase is an S-V split (intermediate position), commas precede and follow the phrase. When the participle phrase is a sentence closer (terminal position), a comma precedes the phrase and a period follows it. (See the sentences above.)

These punctuation guidelines apply only to those participle phrases that are called *nonrestrictive* (the only type practiced in this section). Restrictive participle phrases require no punctuation. Unlike the type we are dealing with here, they are inseparably linked to the noun or pronoun they modify, usually identifying that noun or pronoun rather than adding information about it, as is the case with nonrestrictive participles.

Restrictive

The man **standing by the large tree** is my uncle.

Nonrestrictive

The man, **standing by the large tree**, began yelling.

The type of participle phrase studied in this textbook is nonrestrictive. Although students use both restrictive and nonrestrictive participle phrases, they use the latter far less frequently and need practice to increase that use.

Other

A participle phrase is a removable sentence part; that is, it may be removed without damage to the grammar of the rest of the sentence. This is true only when the participle is not part of a verb phrase.

Here are several pairs of sentences. Each sentence in each pair uses the same participle word. However, in one of the sentences the word is part of a verb phrase; in the other, the word is part of the participle phrase. The presence of the word *was* (or *were*) before the participle indicates that the participle is part of a verb phrase; the absence of the word *was* (or *were*) indicates that the participle is part of a participle phrase.

1a. She **WAS studying French in her room**.
1b. She, **studying French in her room**, didn't answer the phone.
2a. The snow truck **WAS plowing only the main streets**.
2b. **Plowing only the main streets**, the snow truck **WAS working all night**.

Example 1a contains a verb phrase, identified by the presence of *was* immediately before the participle; example 1b contains a participle phrase, identified by the absence of *was* immediately before the participle. Example 2a contains a verb phrase, and 2b contains both a verb phrase (*WAS working all night*) and a participle phrase (*plowing only the main streets*).

It is only the participle phrases that can be removed without damage to the grammar of the rest of the sentence. For example, if you removed the participle phrase from example 2b above, you would still have a grammatical sentence.

The snow truck was working all night. (sentence)

However, if you removed the verb phrase from example 2b, you would not have a grammatical sentence.

Plowing only the main streets, the snow truck. (non-sentence)

Knowing that nonrestrictive participle phrases are removable sentence parts does not deny their importance to a sentence. This knowledge, however, can aid you in identifying them.

PRACTICE 1

Applying the information you have just read, identify each of the boldface phrases below as either a verb phrase or a participle phrase. After identifying each, remove the phrase from the sentence and then classify the remainder as either grammatical (that is, a complete sentence) or ungrammatical (a non-sentence).

1. Away she darted, **stretching close to the ground**.
   Francis Parkman, *The Oregon Trail*

2. The Fog Horn **was blowing steadily**, once every fifteen seconds.
   Ray Bradbury, "The Fog Horn"

3. Some taller buildings push up out of the feathery plain, **topped by rounded caps of air crystals**, like the fur hood Ma wears, only whiter.
   Fritz Leiber, "A Pail of Air"

4. The huge eye on the right side of its anguished head glittered before me like a caldron, into which I might drop, **screaming**.
   Ray Bradbury, "The Fog Horn"

5. Through days of torment he endlessly struggled not to love her; **fearing success**, he escaped it.
   Bernard Malamud, "The Magic Barrel"

6. The old banker **was pacing from corner to corner of his study, recalling to his mind the party he gave in the autumn fifteen years before**.
   Anton Chekov, "The Bet"

The last Practice illustrated the removability of nonrestrictive participle phrases as a means of distinguishing between them and verb phrases, which they somewhat resemble. Another characteristic of participle phrases is their movability within the sentence.

Sometimes repositioning the participle phrase will change the intended meaning, causing what has been traditionally called a dangling participle (or dangling modifier). Here is an original sentence containing two participle phrases plus several variations in which the participle phrases have been moved elsewhere within the sentence.

Original

I could see Catherine, lying on a table, covered by a sheet.
Ernest Hemingway, *A Farewell to Arms*

Variations

Lying on a table, I could see Catherine, covered by a sheet.
I, lying on a table, could see Catherine, covered by a sheet.
Covered by a sheet, I could see Catherine, lying on a table.
I, covered by a sheet, could see Catherine, lying on a table.

All four variations change the intended meaning and are unacceptable. Frequently, however, participle phrases can be moved to other positions with no change in meaning. There are three main positions where participle phrases can be placed: introductory (sentence opener), intermediate (S-V split), and terminal (sentence closer). Here is an original sentence containing a participle phrase plus two variations that result in acceptable repositionings, both faithful to the intended meaning of the original.

Original

Nick fought him against the current, **letting him thump in the water against the spring of the rod**. (terminal)

Ernest Hemingway, "Big Two-Hearted River: Part II"

Variations

Letting him thump in the water against the spring of the rod, Nick fought him against the current. (introductory)

Nick, **letting him thump in the water against the spring of the rod**, fought him against the current. (intermediate)

Which variation to choose depends on the context in which a particular sentence occurs and the position that might better serve the writer's purpose.

PRACTICE 2

Below are original sentences plus variations in which the participle phrases have been repositioned within the sentence. Read the original (the first sentence in each group) carefully to determine the author's intended meaning, especially the noun the participle phrase is intended to modify. Classify each of the variations as either acceptable or unacceptable according to whether the author's intended meaning is retained in the variation. Discuss the reasons for unacceptable variations.

1a. We passed two children, **sobbing and moaning as they ran**.

Peter Abrahams, *Tell Freedom*

  b. **Sobbing and moaning as they ran**, we passed two children.

  c. We, **sobbing and moaning as they ran**, passed two children.

2a. The nurse was with Catherine, who lay on the table, big under the sheet, **looking very pale and tired**.

Ernest Hemingway, *A Farewell to Arms*

  b. The nurse was with Catherine, who lay on the table, **looking very pale and tired**, big under the sheet.

  c. **Looking very pale and tired**, the nurse was with Catherine, who lay on the table, big under the sheet.

  d. The nurse, **looking very pale and tired**, was with Catherine, who lay on the table, big under the sheet.

3a. I watched him leave noiselessly, **moving with a long hip-swinging stride that caused me to frown**.

Ralph Ellison, *Invisible Man*

  b. **Moving with a long hip-swinging stride that caused me to frown**, I watched him leave noiselessly.

c.   I watched him, **moving with a long hip-swinging stride that caused me to frown,** leave noiselessly.

d.   I, **moving with a long hip-swinging stride that caused me to frown,** watched him leave noiselessly.

4a.   Yakov, in loose clothes and peaked cap, was an elongated nervous man with large ears, stained hard hands, a broad back and tormented face, **lightened a bit by gray eyes and brownish hair.**

Bernard Malamud, The Fixer

b.   **Lightened a bit by gray eyes and brownish hair,** Yakov, in loose clothes and peaked cap, was an elongated nervous man with large ears, stained hard hands, a broad back and tormented face.

c.   Yakov, in loose clothes and peaked cap, was an elongated nervous man with large ears, stained hard hands, a broad back and, **lightened a bit by gray eyes and brownish hair,** tormented face.

d.   Yakov, in loose clothes and peaked cap, **lightened a bit by gray eyes and brownish hair,** was an elongated nervous man with large ears, stained hard hands, a broad back and tormented face.

PRACTICE 3

The purpose of this exercise is to give you practice in positioning participles, a skill that helps greatly in achieving sentence structure variety. Rewrite each sentence once, placing the participle phrase in some other position in the sentence where it will be as effective as it was in the original sentence. Punctuate correctly.

1.   The diggers gathered about the rim of the pit, **staring.**

Edmund Ware, "An Underground Episode"

2.   **Frowning,** she pulled her coat closer and shrugged.

Anna Guest, "Beauty Is Truth"

3.   I seemed forever condemned, **ringed by walls.**

Richard Wright, Black Boy

4.   The rockets came like locusts, **swarming and settling in blooms of rosy smoke.**

Ray Bradbury, The Martian Chronicles

5.   **Taking off his cap,** he placed it over the muzzle of his rifle.

Liam O'Flaherty, "The Sniper"

6.   **Crouched on the edge of the plateau,** the schoolmaster looked at the deserted expanse.

Albert Camus, Exile and the Kingdom

7.   We sit down, side by side, **not saying a word for a while.**

Richard E. Kim, Lost Names

8.   **Seated in the gracious shade of a wild tulip tree,** I learned to think that everything has a lesson and a suggestion.

Helen Keller, "The Most Important Day"

9. Up there it looked like a trout stream, **flowing swiftly with shallow stretches and pools under the shadow of the rocks**.

Ernest Hemingway, A Farewell to Arms

10. The all-powerful auto industry, **accustomed to telling the customer what sort of car he wanted**, was suddenly forced to listen for a change.

Jessica Mitford, The American Way of Death

PRACTICE 4

This Practice has two purposes: to reinforce your understanding of the difference between verb phrases and participle phrases, and to give you practice in varying the position of participle phrases you compose.

There are three groups of exercises. For each exercise, write three sentences similar to the models (a, b, c) shown for each group. The first sentence should use the verb phrase (left of slash mark). The second sentence should use the participle phrase (right of slash mark). Underline and label the verb phrase in your first sentence and the participle phrase in your second sentence. (Boldface type is used instead of underlining in the models.) In the third sentence, reposition the participle phrase. Be sure to avoid a dangling participle. Underline and label the participle phrase. Punctuate correctly.

The first group of exercises gives practice in handling present participle phrases (those ending in *ing*). The second group gives practice in handling past participle phrases (those usually ending in *ed* or *en*). The third group gives practice in handling compound participle phrases (two phrases connected by *and*).

Present Participle Phrases

WAS TURNING / TURNING

a. All of a sudden the door at Veek's store **was turning much too fast for people to gain access without danger**. (verb phrase)

b. **Turning much too fast for people to gain access without danger**, the door at Veek's store malfunctioned as a result of a faulty regulator. (participle phrase)

c. The door at Veek's store, **turning much too fast for people to gain access without danger**, malfunctioned as a result of a faulty regulator. (participle phrase)

1. WAS SCREAMING / SCREAMING
2. WAS RUNNING / RUNNING
3. WAS TYPING / TYPING

4. WAS READING / READING
5. WAS THINKING / THINKING

Past Participle Phrases

WAS DRIVEN / DRIVEN

a. The bus **was driven by the woman recently hired by the school board.** (verb phrase)

b. **Driven by the woman recently hired by the school board,** the bus was never late, always had the best attendance, and never had any discipline problems. (participle phrase)

c. The bus, **driven by the woman recently hired by the school board,** was never late, always had the best attendance, and never had any discipline problems. (participle phrase)

6. WAS COVERED / COVERED
7. WAS WRITTEN / WRITTEN
8. WAS TYPED / TYPED
9. WAS RUN / RUN
10. WAS THOUGHT / THOUGHT

Compound Participle Phrases

WAS TROUBLED ... AND WORRIED ... / TROUBLED ... AND WORRIED ...

a. Tony **was troubled by the answer he got and worried that he might not get the job.** (compound verb phrase)

b. Tony, **troubled by the answer he got and worried that he might not get the job,** called his former employer to ask him if he had given him a good reference. (compound participle phrase)

c. **Troubled by the answer he got and worried that he might not get the job,** Tony called his former employer to ask him if he had given him a good reference. (compound participle phrase)

11. WAS WALKING ... AND LOOKING ... / WALKING ... AND LOOKING ...
12. WAS TOURING ... AND BUYING ... / TOURING ... AND BUYING ...
13. WAS RELIEVED ... AND ELATED ... / RELIEVED ... AND ELATED ...

14. WAS DISTURBED . . . AND CONCERNED . . . / DISTURBED . . . AND CONCERNED . . .

15. WAS EXCITED . . . AND HOPING . . . / EXCITED . . . AND HOPING . . .

PRACTICE 5

Each of the professionally written sentences below contains a participle phrase. For each sentence, do the following:

(a) Identify the participle phrase and indicate the type of participle (present or past).

(b) State the position of the phrase (sentence opener, S-V split, or sentence closer).

(c) Punctuate the participle phrase correctly.

1. Being occupied with the misfortune the little round balls had wrought within him the bear gave him no notice.
Jack London, "The Story of Keesh"

2. Manuel lying on the ground kicked at the bull's muzzle with his slippered feet.
Ernest Hemingway, "The Undefeated"

3. Clutching the clawing kitten to her collarbone her hair in her open mouth, she bawled encouragement to them.
Elizabeth Enright, "Nancy"

4. They were diggers in clay transformed by lantern light into a race of giants.
Edmund Ware, "An Underground Episode"

5. Ruthie dressed in a real dress of pink muslin that came below her knees was a little serious in her young-ladiness.
John Steinbeck, *The Grapes of Wrath*

6. A little girl marched stepping neatly over arms and legs she did not look at.
Fritz Leiber, "A Bad Day for Sales"

7. Swinging their grocery bags full of clean watery green onions and odorous liverwurst and red catsup and white bread they would dare each other on past the limits set by their stern mothers.
Ray Bradbury, *The Martian Chronicles*

8. Sometimes a gaggle of them came to the Store filling the whole room chasing out the air and even changing the well-known scents.
Maya Angelou, *I Know Why the Caged Bird Sings*

PRACTICING THE SKILL: SENTENCE SCRAMBLING

Sometimes the positions of participle phrases within a sentence are interchangeable: the same phrase could occur acceptably in any position—introductory, intermediate, or terminal. Which of the three to use will depend on such things as sentence variety, the relative emphasis desired, and the relation of the structure and content of the sentence to the other sentences in the paragraph. Sometimes, however, only two of the three positions (or only one of the three) are acceptable; the other positions would result in unacceptable grammar, poor modification, or lack of emphasis. The following Practice requires you to make the right decision about the positioning of participle phrases.

PRACTICE 6

Unscramble each list of sentence parts three times: first, to produce a sentence with the participle phrase in the introductory position; next, in the intermediate position; and finally, in the terminal position. Classify the use of each position as either acceptable or unacceptable. If two positions are acceptable, or if all three are acceptable, discuss which position you prefer. Punctuate correctly.

1a. was waiting on the landing outside

  b. Bernard

  c. wearing a black turtleneck sweater, dirty flannels, and slippers

Brian Moore, The Lonely Passion of Judith Hearne

2a. could see the lake

  b. sitting up in bed eating breakfast

  c. we

  d. and the mountains across the lake on the French side

Ernest Hemingway, A Farewell to Arms

3a. coming down the pole

  b. with no control over my movements

  c. had a sense

  d. I

  e. of being whirled violently through the air

Richard E. Byrd, Alone

4a. black

  b. a little house

  c. perched on high piles

  d. in the distance

  e. appeared

Joseph Conrad, Tales of Unrest

5a. screaming and begging to be allowed to go with her mother

  b. when we had made our way downstairs

  c. saw the woman with the lovely complexion

d. Miss Pilzer

e. we

Gerda Weissmann Klein, *All But My Life*

When a sentence contains two or more participle phrases, the phrases are called "compound."

Examples of Compound Participle Phrases

He strode forward, **crushing ants with each step** and **brushing them off his clothes,** till he stood above the skeleton, which lay sprawled under a small bush.

Doris Lessing, *African Stories*

In the sentence above, two participle phrases are joined by the coordinating conjunction *and.* Below the two consecutive participle phrases are joined with a comma.

My mother is waiting, and I nearly run into her, **choking with pounding, aching emotions, trembling with a dizzy swirl of ecstasy and fear.**

Richard E. Kim, *Lost Names*

PRACTICE 7

Each of the scrambled sentences below contains compound participle phrases. Unscramble each to produce the most effective arrangement of the sentence parts. Punctuate correctly. Decide the best order in which to arrange participle phrases that occur in series. When you finish, compare your sentences with the original in the References. How does yours differ? Which do you like better? Why?

1a. with the cautious, half-furtive effort of the sightless

b. and thumping his way before him

c. he was a blind beggar

d. carrying the traditional battered cane

MacKinlay Kantor, "A Man Who Had No Eyes"

2a. all had the look of invalids crawling into the hospital on their last legs

b. the passengers

c. blinking their eyes against the blinding sunlight

d. emerging from the mildewed dimness of the customs sheds

Katherine Anne Porter, *Ship of Fools*

3a. as long as possible

b. and so we went to the station

c. trying to be together

d. taking the longer way

e. across the meadow

Gerda Weissmann Klein, All But My Life

4a. and yet knowing no way to avoid it

b. that winter my mother and brother came

c. buying furniture on the installment plan

d. and we set up housekeeping

e. being cheated

Richard Wright, Black Boy

5a. as Dave called them

b. instead of sleeping that night

c. severing the leaders

d. we pored over the schematic diagrams of her structures

e. tracing the thoughts through mazes of her wiring

f. implanting heterones

Lester del Rey, "Helen O'Loy"

6a. where George Willard sat listening

b. and breaking off the tale

c. Doctor Parcival

d. in the office of the *Winesburg Eagle*

e. jumping to his feet

f. began to walk up and down

Sherwood Anderson, Winesburg, Ohio

7a. came up slowly

b. his long embroidered robe streaming over her arm almost to the ground

c. a young Mexican woman

d. dressed in the elegant, perpetual mourning of her caste

e. who carried her baby

f. softened and dispirited by recent childbirth

g. leaning on the arm of the Indian nurse

Katherine Anne Porter, Ship of Fools

8a. bewildered by the numbers

b. wiping, daubing, winding

c. tugged here and there in his stockinged feet

d. Dr. Sasaki lost all sense of profession

e. he became an automaton

f. staggered by so much raw flesh

g. and stopped working as a skillful surgeon

h. and a sympathetic man

i. mechanically wiping, daubing, winding

John Hersey, Hiroshima

PRACTICING THE SKILL: SENTENCE IMITATING

In the sentence below from Stephen Crane's *The Red Badge of Courage* (the opening sentence of the novel), the use of a participle is not simply a frill to add a little sentence variety. Its use, and especially its placement at the end of the sentence, is crucial to the understanding of the central character of the story, the youth named Henry Fleming.

The cold passed reluctantly from the earth, and the retiring fogs revealed an army stretched out on the hills, **resting.**

That the army is resting, not fighting, is emphasized and underscores the youth's romantic misconception about what actually goes on in war. When Henry enlisted, he thought that war would bring excitement and glory, not boredom and "resting." Thus Crane, in using the participle "resting" to end the sentence, implies at the very outset of the novel that in human life there is often a difference between expectation and realization, an irony that relates significantly to the major theme of the novel.

Such purposeful uses of participles are the mark of a skilled writer. In this part of the book you will be focusing on other examples and imitating them, noticing especially how the writers of the examples use participles to achieve specific effects. Compare Crane's sentence with the following:

The headache began suddenly after the conference, and the growing pain saturated his body stuck there amid the cocktail chatter, **aching.**

This sentence is an imitation of Crane's structure. Like Crane's, it contains a participle in the emphatic terminal position.

PRACTICE 8

Underneath the model sentence are three imitations. Both the model and the imitations contain participles. The imitations are presented as a list of scrambled sentence parts for you to unscramble to duplicate the structure of the model. The first imitation uses nonsense language for content; it will help you focus your attention on structural similarities between the scrambled sentence and the model. The two other imitations use sense language. Unscramble each of the three sentences to produce a sentence similar in structure to the model. In addition, identify the sentence parts in the scrambled list that are participle phrases.

Model

As he ran away into the darkness, they repented of their weakness and ran after him, swearing and throwing sticks and great balls of soft mud at the figure that screamed and ran faster and faster into the darkness.

Sherwood Anderson, *Winesburg, Ohio*

Scrambled Nonsense Imitation

1a. who flurded and narred cranster and cranster over the frame

b. and turling stews and red bleeps of wrinkled networks to the morm

c. and purted about them

d. when they fusted nearby in a zurner

e. smiling

f. he confrusticated about his nestings

Scrambled Sense Imitation

2a. as her arm whirled fast over the egg-whites

b. and stared at it

c. and expressing confusion and frustration over the third direction in the recipe

d. her face shifted toward the cookbook

e. grimacing

f. that listed and explained more and ever more of the procedure

Scrambled Sense Imitation

3a. stretching

b. that beckoned but hid farther and farther from his reach

c. after Jo-Jo climbed higher onto the counter

d. but missing jars and boxes in the rear with bright colors

e. he pulled on the doors

f. and looked for the candy

PRACTICE 9

The model sentence here is broken into the six sentence parts that you un-scrambled, arranged in the same order in which they occur in the model. For each part from the model, list the equivalent part from each of the scrambled versions. After providing the equivalent sentence parts, write two of your own sentences imitating the model, one sentence part at a time.

First Sentence Part

Model: As he ran away into the darkness,

Second Sentence Part

Model: they repented of their weakness

Third Sentence Part

Model: and ran after him,

Fourth Sentence Part (Participle)

Model: swearing

Fifth Sentence Part (Participle)

Model: and throwing sticks and great balls of soft mud at the figure

Sixth Sentence Part

Model: that screamed and ran faster and faster into the darkness.

PRACTICE 10

This Practice will review participles as well as provide examples of imitations of models. Later Practices, in which you do the imitating, will be easier for having done this exercise.

First, read the model sentence carefully, paying special attention to the structure: position, type, and number of sentence parts; punctuation; and so forth. Next, read through the three sentences underneath the model and, again paying special attention to the parts of each of the three sentences, identify the one sentence that is an imitation of the model.

This Practice contains nonsense language that will make it easier for you to focus primarily on the *way* and not the *what* of the sentence: the structure, not the content.

In each model the participle phrase is in boldface.

1.   *Model:* Their meeps, **kacking near the zoot torps of jangles,** zinked up now and then brask glanes of far tanies.

A.   Its canted broop and masting tree, a short spittle with maple heads, veered once and then, slowing fast, got stripes.

B.   Their zap, neeking over the calt meems of apples, mulled out once or twice star camps with new yoorts.

C.   Their noot, blumper and shringingly sleek, a fine style of auto, began to sittle over a flame, shining green.

2.   *Model:* **Trying to crink some noons for the pinched nails,** Weemie saw, **harping slowly near the cringed flake of the smoke,** a rug with some curders.

A.   Gying over a sturdy green flapper when day is drawn feeply is not, of course, the best munchion to sabure a kettle, even one with feathers.

B.   Buking when the samors, trying to stipe a flattened hootalator, ascended, the lead minch towly matted a lesson plan, inch by inch in jugs.

C.   Jaloping to breest a cookie in three minutes, Bamp wooped, swimming dryly by the back grass of mirror, some pretzels with nipies.

3.   *Model:* By the black, **easing near some iotas which they had been making oranges**, they had been narted with ten mudled yamies but steamed near the sarses in a flash, where Jert, **crandled in colored airs**, but smart as a goon with his peached pencil, was sleeping stories in a telephone tent.

A.   A new sport, called a breeming discovery by the world of high brown lows, one they had been gristing with for over millions of interminable blue seconds, is, some think, crandled with two of top hairs, but swift as the proverbial steek, who always is finding bread in wind and fresh buttons.

B.   Toward midnight, heening down from the hotel where they had been greebing stotas, they had been wusted by some crayed bevellers and brawn into the soup by the sauter, where Zeek, cloned by grape mountains, and slick as a shoe under his roisting snow, was clocking mews over a shreeded popcorn.

C.   A foned blast, a gerunding of the parts of the clowing infinitive, the confrusticated grammar teacher howled in the kernels, where some strayed morphemes, enclosed in silence and written in air, certain of the infinity of finitude in linguistics, were treed in diagrams of crystal fog.

If you were able to pick out the imitation of the model, you saw that structure, like content, is something you can *read*. Noticing structure, both in the sentences of professional writers and in your own, is an important skill to develop—one that will help you write mature sentences easily.

PRACTICE 11

Now that you are familiar with the structure of the model sentences from the previous Practice, your work here will be simple. In this Practice, write two sentence imitations for each of the three models in the previous Practice, using their sentence structure but providing your own content.

Each sentence below is the original of the nonsense models in the last Practice. First, tell which sentence matches which model. Then, write two imitations: a nonsense imitation and a sense imitation. The participles are in boldface.

1.   **Pretending to take an interest in the New Season's Models**, Gumbril made, **squinting sideways over the burning tip of his cigar**, an inventory of her features.

Aldous Huxley, Antic Hay

2. Toward sunset, **coming down from the mountain where he had been felling timber,** he had been caught by some strayed revellers and drawn into the group by the lake, where Mattie, **encircled by facetious youths,** and bright as a blackberry under her spreading hat, was brewing coffee over a gipsy fire.
Edith Wharton, *Ethan Frome*

3. Its rays, **shining upon the moving masses of troops,** brought forth here and there sudden gleams of silver or gold.
Stephen Crane, *The Red Badge of Courage*

PRACTICE 12

In this last Practice on sentence imitating using participles, you can test your ability to imitate model sentences with only the aid of the model.

The model sentences are arranged in three groups according to the position of the participle. Following the structure of the model sentence, but using your own content, write a sentence imitation for each of the models below. Imitate the structure of the entire sentence, not just the participle phrase.

Introductory Participle Phrases (Sentence Openers)

1. **Taking off his cap,** he placed it over the muzzle of his rifle.
Liam O'Flaherty, "The Sniper"

2. **Walking forward, watching the bull's feet,** he saw successively his eyes, his wet muzzle, and the wide, forward-pointing spread of his horns.
Ernest Hemingway, "The Undefeated"

3. **Sitting beside his flowering window while the panes rattled and the wind blew in under the door,** Rosicky gave himself to reflection as he had not done since those Sundays in the loft of the furniture factory in New York, long ago.
Willa Cather, "Neighbor Rosicky"

4. **Regarding death thus out of the corner of his eye,** he conceived it to be nothing but rest, and he was filled with a momentary astonishment that he should have made an extraordinary commotion over the mere matter of getting killed.
Stephen Crane, *The Red Badge of Courage*

Intermediate Participle Phrases (S-V Splits)

5. The turkeys, **roosting in the tree out of coyotes' reach,** clicked drowsily.
John Steinbeck, *The Red Pony*

6. Her brown face, **upraised,** was stained with tears.
Stephen Crane, *The Red Badge of Courage*

7. On September 23 the commissioners, **riding in Army ambulances from Fort Robinson and escorted by a somewhat enlarged cavalry troop,** again arrived at the council shelter.
Dee Brown, *Bury My Heart at Wounded Knee*

8.   Mr. Braxton Underwood, who had been sitting quietly in a chair reserved for the Press, **soaking up testimony with his sponge of a brain,** allowed his eyes to rove over the colored balcony, and they met mine.

Harper Lee, To Kill a Mockingbird

Terminal Participle Phrases (Sentence Closers)

9.   This land was waterless, **furred with the cacti which could store water and with the great-rooted brush which could reach deep into the earth for a little moisture and get along on very little.**

John Steinbeck, The Pearl

10.   There was good air and light, and I worked quite hard, **skipping rope, shadow-boxing, doing abdominal exercises lying on the floor in a patch of sunlight that came through the open window, and occasionally scaring the professor when we boxed.**

Ernest Hemingway, A Farewell to Arms

11.   He hung around L.A., **broke most of the time, working as an usher in movie theatres, getting an occasional part as an extra on the lots or a bit on TV, dreaming and yearning and hungry, eating cold spaghetti out of the can.**

John Dos Passos, "The Sinister Adolescents"

12.   Nothing else in the world would do but the pure waters which had been summoned from the lakes far away and the sweet fields of grassy dew on early morning, **lifted to the open sky, carried in laundered dusters, nine hundred miles brushed with wind, electrified with high voltage, and condensed upon cool air.**

Ray Bradbury, Vintage Bradbury

Multiple Positions

13.   She, **thrilled and in part seduced by his words,** instead of resisting as definitely as she would have in any other case, now gazed at him, **fascinated by his enthusiasms.**

Theodore Dreiser, An American Tragedy

14.   Al, **bending over the wheel,** kept shifting eyes from the road to the instrument panel, **watching the ammeter needle,** which jerked suspiciously, **watching the oil gauge and the heat indicator.**

John Steinbeck, The Grapes of Wrath

15.   A few stray white bread crumbs lay on the cleanly washed floor by the table; **putting the lamp upon a low stool,** he began to pick up the crumbs, **carrying them to his mouth one by one with unbelievable rapidity.**

Sherwood Anderson, Winesburg, Ohio

16.   **Soiled by the filth of a strange city, spat upon by unknown mouths, driven from the streets into the roadway,** where, a human beast of burden, he pursued his work, a porter, **carrying the heaviest loads upon his back, scurrying between carriages, carts, and horses, staring death in the eyes every moment,** he still kept silent.

Isaac Peretz, "Bontsha the Silent"

PRACTICING THE SKILL: SENTENCE COMBINING

In this part you'll produce single sentences from lists derived from sentences by professional writers. Each of the original sentences contains a participle phrase. In the References are the original sentences for you to compare with yours. In sentence combining you have to make more choices about sentence structure than you did in sentence imitating. Here, you must decide what form or structure to give a list of sentences as you combine them into just one sentence.

PRACTICE 13

In one of the sentences in each group, a slash mark (/) indicates that the original sentence has a participle phrase at that place. Combine the sentences underneath into a participle phrase that will fit smoothly into the place. Write an imitation of the resulting sentence, using your own content and the structure of the model. For example:

Sentence One: The little shack, the rattling, rotting barn were gray-bitten with sea salt, / .
Sentence Two: The shack and the barn were beaten.
Sentence Three: They were beaten by the damp wind.
Sentence Four: This happened until they had taken on the color.
Sentence Five: The color was of the granite hills.

Combination with Participle Phrase

The little shack, the rattling, rotting barn were gray-bitten with sea salt, **beaten by the damp wind until they had taken on the color of the granite hills**.
John Steinbeck, "Flight"

Imitation

The team manager, the surprised, elated team were encouraged, **roused by the roaring fans after the opposing team had fumbled on the fifty-yard line during the last play**.

1a. / , I was wet, cold, and very hungry.
 b. I was lying on the floor.
 c. The floor was of the flat-car.
 d. I was lying with the guns beside me.
 e. The guns were under the canvas.
   Based on a sentence by Ernest Hemingway, *A Farewell to Arms*

2a. The trail moved up the dry shale hillside, / , / , / . (three participle phrases)
 b. The trail was avoiding rocks.

c. It was dropping under clefts.

d. It was climbing in and out of something.

e. The something was old water scars.
Based on a sentence by John Steinbeck, "Flight"

3a. There was a tattered man, / , who trudged quietly at the youth's side.

b. He was fouled with dust.

c. He was fouled with blood.

d. He was fouled with powder stain.

e. He was fouled from hair to shoes.
Based on a sentence by Stephen Crane, *The Red Badge of Courage*

4a. I brought the boat up to the stone pier, and the barman pulled in the line, / and / . (two participle phrases)

b. The barman was coiling it.

c. The coiling was on the bottom of the boat.

d. The barman was hooking the spinner on the edge.

e. The edge was of the gunwale.
Based on a sentence by Ernest Hemingway, *A Farewell to Arms*

PRACTICE 14

Below you are given a model sentence and a list of sentences to be combined to resemble the structure of the model. In addition to practicing the use of participles, you will practice other sentence composing skills used by the authors of the model sentences. You may not know the names of the other skills, but you will be able to imitate them if you follow the directions for this Practice. The names aren't important; your use of the skills is.

First, read the model several times, paying special attention to the structure of the sentence. In each model the participle phrase is in boldface. Study it and the rest of the sentence carefully; you'll need to be familiar with not only the participle phrase but also the rest of the sentence structure.

Next, read the list of sentences underneath the model. Combine these into one sentence having basically the same structure as the model. The order in which the sentences are listed is the order of the parts of the model. In other words, convert the first sentence into the first sentence part of the model, the second sentence into the second part, and so forth.

Finally, write an imitation of the model, keeping the same structure but providing your own content. For example:

Model

The horse found the entrance to the trail where it left the flat and started up, **stumbling and slipping on the rocks.**
John Steinbeck, "Flight"

Sentences to Be Converted	*Conversions*
1. The cycle hit something.	1. The cycle hit
2. It hit a stretch.	2. a stretch
3. The stretch was of ice.	3. of ice
4. It happened as it rounded the bend.	4. as it rounded the bend
5. In addition, it slid sideways.	5. and slid sideways,
6. Then it was tottering.	6. tottering
7. In addition, then it was veering.	7. and veering
8. It was veering toward the shoulder.	8. toward the shoulder.

Imitation

His arm contacted the concrete of the schoolyard after he missed the jump and landed hard, **snapping and breaking at the impact**.

Here are the three sentences with their equivalent sentence parts.

Model	*Combination*	*Imitation*
1. The horse found	1. The cycle hit	1. His arm contacted
2. the entrance	2. a stretch	2. the concrete
3. to the trail	3. of ice	3. of the schoolyard
4. where it left the flat	4. as it rounded the bend	4. after he missed the jump
5. and started up,	5. and slid sideways,	5. and landed hard,
6. stumbling	6. tottering	6. snapping
7. and slipping	7. and veering	7. and breaking
8. on the rocks.	8. toward the shoulder.	8. at the impact.

Here are the three sentences from this example: same structure, different content. Participle phrases are in boldface.

Model

The horse found the entrance to the trail where it left the flat and started up, **stumbling and slipping on the rocks**.

Combination

The cycle hit a stretch of ice as it rounded the bend and slid sideways, **tottering and veering toward the shoulder**.

Imitation

His arm contacted the concrete of the schoolyard after he missed the jump and landed hard, **snapping and breaking at the impact**.

Convert one sentence at a time into a structure resembling the equivalent part of the model sentence. Continue until you have converted all the sentences into such structures.

A.   *Model:* The sound of monotonous ax blows rang through the forest, and the insects, **nodding upon their perches**, crooned like old women.
Stephen Crane, The Red Badge of Courage

1.   A pile of new debris was doing something.
2.   It cluttered up the driveway.
3.   In addition, the tenants were gazing at the disgrace.
4.   They watched with heavy hearts.

B.   *Model:* He stood there, his coat wet, **holding his wet hat**, and said nothing.
Ernest Hemingway, A Farewell to Arms

1.   The dog did something.
2.   He sat up.
3.   His mouth was clenching the rolled newspaper.
4.   He was wagging his tail.
5.   In addition, he begged a reward.

C.   *Model:* The little shack, the rattling, rotting barn were gray-bitten with sea salt, **beaten by the damp wind until they had taken on the color of the granite hills**.
John Steinbeck, "Flight"

1.   Something had been done to the upholstered pieces.
2.   Something had been done to the expensive, polished tables.
3.   They had been moved into the huge dining room.
4.   They were covered with endless painter's cloths.
5.   This was done so that they would be protected.
6.   The protection was from the splatterings of paint.

D.   *Model:* The strength that had been as a miracle in her body left, and she half-reeled across the floor, **clutching at the back of the chair in which she had spent so many long days staring out over the tin roofs into the main street of Winesburg**.
Sherwood Anderson, Winesburg, Ohio

1. The meeting had been like something.
2. It had been like a marathon among meetings.
3. The meeting continued.
4. In addition, the leader deliberated about his strategy.
5. He was stalling after the last remarks from the representative.
6. The representative was the one with whom he had planned something.
7. What they had planned were so many emergency ploys focusing upon every conceivable tactic.
8. The tactic was for the suppression of the opposition.

PRACTICE 15

Combine each list of sentences into one sentence containing a participle phrase. Underline each phrase. You may eliminate words and change their form as long as the intended meaning remains. Punctuate correctly. When you finish, compare your sentences with the original sentences in the References.

1a. He was bleeding profusely.
b. In addition, he was cut off from his supply of eagles' blood.
c. He had never been closer to death.
Based on a sentence by J. D. Salinger, *Nine Stories*

2a. The trail moved up the dry shale hillside.
b. It was avoiding rocks.
c. It was dropping under clefts.
d. It was climbing in old water scars.
e. In addition, it was climbing out of old water scars.
Based on a sentence by John Steinbeck "Flight"

3a. He accepted new environment.
b. He accepted, in addition, new circumstance.
c. He accepted both with great coolness.
d. He was eating from his haversack.
e. He was eating at every opportunity.
Based on a sentence by Stephen Crane, *The Red Badge of Courage*

4a. The farm building huddled like something.
b. It huddled like the clinging aphids on the mountain skirts.
c. It was crouched low to the ground.
d. It was as though something might happen.
e. What might happen is that the wind might blow them into the sea.
Based on a sentence by John Steinbeck, "Flight"

5a. His face was fleshy.
b. His face was, in addition, pallid.
c. His face was touched with colour.
d. The colour was only at two places.
e. One place was at the thick hanging lobes of his ears.
f. Another place was at the wide wings of his nose.
Based on a sentence by James Joyce, "The Dead"

6a. I pulled.
b. I raised.
c. I leaned forward.
d. I found the water.
e. I dipped and pulled.
f. I was rowing.
g. The rowing was done as easily as I could.
Based on a sentence by Ernest Hemingway, *A Farewell to Arms*

7a. By and by, one group after another came straggling back.
b. They came straggling back to the mouth of the cave.
c. They were panting.
d. They were hilarious.
e. They were smeared from head to foot with tallow drippings.
f. They were daubed with clay.
g. In addition, they were entirely delighted with the success of the day.
Based on a sentence by Mark Twain, *The Adventures of Tom Sawyer*

8a. Adolph Knipe took a sip of stout.
b. He was tasting the malty-bitter flavor.
c. He was feeling the trickle of cold liquid.
d. He felt the trickle as it traveled down his throat.
e. He felt the trickle, in addition, as it settled in the top of his stomach.
f. At the top of his stomach it was cool at first.
g. It was then spreading and becoming warm.
h. It was making a little area of warmness inside him.
Based on a sentence by Roald Dahl, "The Great Automatic Grammatisator"

PRACTICING THE SKILL: SENTENCE EXPANDING

In this part (unlike in the previous parts on sentence scrambling, sentence imitating, and sentence combining) you have to supply both the structure and *the content* without any help from model sentences. You are doing almost all of the work on your own, unaided by models. Your ability to expand sentences by using participles can be a strong indicator of how well you can add this skill permanently to your writing style.

In all of the sentence expanding Practices, follow the same guidelines. First, select content that blends well with the content of the author's sentence. Second, express that content through participle phrases. Punctuate correctly.

PRACTICE 16

Add a participle phrase to each of the reduced sentences below, blending your content with the rest of the sentence. Each of the sentences (in its original, complete version) had a participle phrase in the place indicated by the slash mark. When you finish, compare your sentence with the original in the References.

Reduced Sentence

She ate well, / , and pressed a second helping of beans on Jotham Powell, whose wants she generally ignored.

Student-Expanded Sentence

She ate well, **attempting to nourish her body back to its usual good health while her mind with its peculiar sickness went unnourished,** and pressed a second helping of beans on Jotham Powell, whose wants she generally ignored.

Original Sentence by Author

She ate well, **declaring that the mild weather made her feel better,** and pressed a second helping of beans on Jotham Powell, whose wants she generally ignored.

Edith Wharton, *Ethan Frome*

Practice a variety of lengths and degrees of modification for your participle phrases. Don't be disappointed if your content is unlike that of the original. In sentence expanding, you're not trying to imitate. You're trying to imagine both content and structure (participle phrase) that will work well when blended with the rest of the author's sentence.

1.   It was early in April in the year '83 that I woke one morning to find Sherlock Holmes standing, / , by the side of my bed.
From a sentence by Sir Arthur Conan Doyle, "The Speckled Band"

2.   Presently the dawn began to break, and the sky to the east grew yellow and red, / .
From a sentence by Winston S. Churchill, "I Escape from the Boers"

3.   The children crawled over the shelves and into the potato and onion bins, / .
From a sentence by Maya Angelou, *I Know Why the Caged Bird Sings*

4.   And he, / , at once looked over his shoulder at her and, / , signaled that he would meet her.

From a sentence by Theodore Dreiser, *An American Tragedy*

5.   In the late afternoon, the truck came back, / and / , and there was a layer of dust in the bed, and the hood was covered with dust, and the headlights were obscured with a red flour.

From a sentence by John Steinbeck, *The Grapes of Wrath*

6.   He stood there, / and / , / .

From a sentence by Roald Dahl, "Beware of the Dog"

7.   The people, / , waved and shrieked happily, / , / , / , / , / .

From a sentence by Ray Bradbury, *Martian Chronicles*

PRACTICE 17

In the last Practice, the length of the participle phrases you added to the authors' sentences was your choice. Here, try to add approximately the same number of words that the authors used for their participle phrases. The number of words in the original participle phrase, including modification within the phrase, is indicated next to the slash mark. Most of the participle phrases in the original sentences are long and highly modified. In the following example from Sherwood Anderson's *Winesburg, Ohio*, notice how Anderson achieves his highly modified participle phrase. The participle is capitalized; the modifiers are in boldface.

The coming of industrialism, **ATTENDED by all the roar and rattle of affairs, the shrill cries of millions of new voices that have come among us from overseas, the going and coming of trains, the growth of cities, the building of the inter-urban car lines that weave in and out of towns and past farm-houses, and now in these later days the coming of automobiles,** has worked a tremendous change in the lives and in the habits of thought of our people of Mid-America.

Even for a professional writer, the participle phrase is extremely long, longer than those you will be expected to write; however, it is a good example of the possibilities for expanding participle phrases. Most of the sentence is contained in the participle phrase. The rest (the one main clause in the sentence) is relatively simple.

The coming of industrialism has worked a tremendous change in the lives and in the habits of thought of our people of Mid-America.

Remember, add content that blends smoothly with the rest of the author's sentence, using a highly modified participle phrase that meets or exceeds the number of words next to the slash mark.

The participle from the author's participle phrase is provided to get you started. You provide the modifiers.

1. Soon the men began to gather, /4 SURVEYING ..., /8 SPEAK-ING. ...

From a sentence by Shirley Jackson, "The Lottery"

2. Flaherty even now was calling for his wife, /4 BUYING ..., /15 FILLING. ...

From a sentence by Irwin Shaw, "The Eighty-Yard Run"

3. With the core of the reel showing, his heart feeling stopped with excitement, /10 LEANING ..., Nick thumbed the reel hard with his left hand.

From a sentence by Ernest Hemingway, "Big Two-Hearted River"

4. As she peered inside, with her legs apart and her hands on her knees, she whistled, unmelodically, through her teeth, /12 KEEPING. ...

From a sentence by J. D. Salinger, *Nine Stories*

5. The train stopped in Vevey, then went on, /22 PASSING. ...

From a sentence by Ernest Hemingway, *A Farewell to Arms*

6. I stayed well out in the lake, /2 ROWING ..., /2 RESTING ... and /10 HOLDING. ...

From a sentence by Ernest Hemingway, *A Farewell to Arms*

7. Mrs. Carpenter was putting sun-tan oil on Sybil's shoulders, /11 SPREADING. ...

From a sentence by J. D. Salinger, *Nine Stories*

8. Lil, who would probably be just outside the gate with her boy, would hear Father's voice and hurry in, /8 KNOWING ..., and almost as soon as she entered the kitchen she would be greeted with a fist or a lifted boot, and soon her rouge and mascara would be mingled with tears and blood as she wilted under a cascade of senseless violence, /7 not KNOWING ..., /13 KNOWING. ...

From a sentence by Christy Brown, *Down All the Days*

5
Reviewing and Applying Sentence Composing Skills

In the preceding sections of the book you learned to identify, punctuate, and use structures that are frequently used by professional writers but rarely used by students. The purpose was to provide extensive practice in the use of those structures so that their use would become more spontaneous and natural—and therefore more frequent—in your own writing.

The purpose of this section is to practice using the structures (absolute, appositive, and participle phrases) in a variety of ways. Even though many of these Practices may seem easy, it's essential that you do each, for repeated practice is necessary for the structures to become an automatic part of your writing style.

PRACTICE 1

The items in the list below are not sentences; they are fragments of sentences. Each fragment consists of a noun followed by an absolute, appositive, or participle phrase. Tell which of the three follows each noun and explain the reasons for your identification.

1. Willy Loman, **believing the illusion that his life has been a success and that his popularity is unexcelled,** . . . .
2. Finny, **the object of Gene's ambivalence,** . . . .
3. Hester, **shouting at her daughter Pearl who stood defiantly on the other side of the creek,** . . . .
4. Harry, **the fictional representative of his creator Ernest Hemingway,** . . . .
5. Bartleby, **his enigmatic answer implicitly challenging the limits of his employer's patience and charity,** . . . .

6. Huck Finn, governed only by the law written on his heart in his decision to save Jim, ...

7. Laura, the lovely, timid cripple whose fragility matches that of her beloved glass unicorn, ...

8. John Proctor, his dilemma resolved by his decision to sacrifice his life rather than lose his good name, ...

PRACTICE 2

Each sentence below contains an absolute, appositive, or participle phrase. Identify which in each case.

1. Now, facing the bull, he was conscious of many things at the same time.
Ernest Hemingway, "The Undefeated"

2. The writer, an old man with a white mustache, had some difficulty in getting into bed.
Sherwood Anderson, *Winesburg, Ohio*

3. Crouched on the edge of the plateau, the schoolmaster looked at the deserted expanse.
Albert Camus, *Exile and the Kingdom*

4. His head aching, his throat sore, he forgot to light the cigarette.
Sinclair Lewis, *Cass Timberlane*

5. He stood quivering, stiff ears forward, eyes rolling so that the whites showed, ...
John Steinbeck, *The Red Pony*

6. About the bones ants were ebbing away, their pincers full of meat.
Doris Lessing, *African Stories*

7. I went over and took a teakwood chair with cushions of emerald-green silk, sitting stiffly with my brief case across my knees.
Ralph Ellison, *Invisible Man*

8. A little house, perched on high piles, appeared black in the distance.
Joseph Conrad, *Tales of Unrest*

9. One of eleven brothers and sisters, Harriet was a moody, willful child.
Langston Hughes, "Road to Freedom"

10. Buck stood and looked on, the successful champion, the dominant primordial beast who had made his kill and found it good.
Jack London, *Call of the Wild*

11. Her gaze, deceiving, transforming her to her imaginings, changed the contour of her sallow-skinned face, re-fashioning her long pointed nose on which a small chilly tear had gathered.
Brian Moore, *The Lonely Passion of Judith Hearne*

12. Once Enoch Bentley, the older one of the boys, struck his father, old Tom Bentley, with the butt of a teamster's whip, and the old man seemed likely to die.
Sherwood Anderson, *Winesburg, Ohio*

PRACTICE 3

Try playing "The Appositive Game" to help you review appositive phrases. The procedure is quite simple. Divide the class into two teams. Each member of each team writes down an appositive phrase that identifies a famous person, fictional or nonfictional: a politician, an actor, a character from literature, an athlete, a singer, and so forth. Each appositive phrase must be at least fifteen words long. When a member of the team reads an appositive phrase, any member of the other team may guess the identity, but no more than one guess may be made. Scoring is as follows: if the identification of the famous person is *not* an appositive phrase, that team loses one point; if the opposing team correctly identifies the person described by the appositive phrase, that team gains one point. The team with the most points at the end of two rounds is the winner. For example:

Description of Famous Person (an appositive phrase that must contain at least fifteen words)

a popular superhero whose story has been told through radio, television, and movies and whose alter-ego is that of a mild-mannered reporter for a newspaper

Answer: Superman

PRACTICE 4

Here you will compose one sentence using a series of appositive and participle phrases, all expressed in parallel structure.

The purpose of the sentence is to describe vividly four of your former teachers, each of whom will be identified by both an appositive phrase and a participle phrase.

In addition to reviewing the uses of appositive and participle phrases, you will review the use of the colon to introduce a list and the semicolon to separate items in a list when the items themselves contain commas. (You may want to review the uses of colons and semicolons in the section on punctuation at the beginning of this textbook.)

Begin your sentence with the following main clause, followed by a colon to introduce the list of descriptions.

Main Clause

Main Clause: I can never forget these four teachers, each of whom had a certain specialness: (*list*)

For each teacher, provide in order the teacher's name, an appositive phrase, and a participle phrase (both phrases describing that teacher). Remember to put a comma before and after each appositive phrase and a semicolon after each participle phrase. For example:

Mrs. Britton, a strict but fair woman who demanded good behavior, hauling kids off to the book room for punishment; (*and so forth*).

PRACTICE 5

In the following series of tasks, you will review absolute, appositive, and participle phrases, noticing their differences, uses, and positions.

Task One

Select a noun. Next to it write an absolute phrase. Using the same noun, write an appositive phrase. Again using the same noun, write a participle phrase. Put commas before and after the phrases. For example:

1.   The handyman, **his tools randomly scattered over the workbench,** (*absolute*)
2.   The handyman, **an elderly, neat gentleman with never a grease stain on his work clothes,** (*appositive*)
3.   The handyman, **painting over last year's paint on the old lawn furniture,** (*participle*)

Task Two

Write three sentences, using for part of the content the material you produced in task one. Add appropriate content to complete each sentence. For example:

1a.   The handyman, **his tools randomly scattered over the workbench,** tried to make a little order out of the mess by putting all like things together.
2a.   The handyman, **an elderly, neat gentleman with never a grease stain on his work clothes,** told the distraught housewife that in just a few minutes he would have things under control.
3a.   The handyman, **painting over last year's paint on the old lawn furniture,** noticed a paint bubble, got out a straight pin, pricked it, scraped the loose paint away, then sanded it smooth.

Task Three

The three structures can frequently be placed in other positions in relation to the nouns they refer to. To practice moving them, rewrite the sentences from task two by placing the phrases in the sentence opener (introductory) position. In task two they were in the S-V split (intermediate) position. When the structures are in the introductory position, a comma is used after the phrase. For example:

1b.   **His tools randomly scattered over the workbench,** the handyman tried to make a little order out of the mess by putting all like things together. (*introductory absolute*)

2b.   **An elderly, neat gentleman with never a grease stain on his work clothes,** the handyman told the distraught housewife that in just a few minutes he would have things under control. (*introductory appositive*)

3b.   **Painting over last year's paint on the old lawn furniture,** the handyman noticed a paint bubble, got out a straight pin, pricked it, scraped the loose paint away, then sanded it smooth. (*introductory participle*)

Task Four

The structures may also occur in the sentence closer (terminal) position. To practice their use in this position, retain the three phrases from the above tasks, but write new content for the rest of each sentence. Place whatever noun you are working with from the preceding tasks immediately before the phrases. When the structures are in the terminal position, a comma is used before the phrase. For example:

1c.   Mr. Farley, overseer for landscaping and exteriors at Smithton Estates, criticized the sloppiness of the painter's shed in the maintenance building, and all the while nearby was the handyman, **his tools randomly scattered over the workbench**. (*terminal absolute*)

2c.   After ruling out the cook, the baby-sitter, and the boy who cut their lawn, they decided that, with their unfortunate fallen financial state, they could only keep in their hire the handyman, **an elderly, neat gentleman with never a grease stain on his work clothes**. (*terminal appositive*)

3c.   While she was stretching the lace curtains out in the backyard, he was putting old clothes in boxes to give to Goodwill; and paying no attention to either was the handyman, **painting over last year's paint on the old lawn furniture**. (*terminal participle*)

Task Five

Now that you have practiced the three positions in which the structures may occur (introductory, intermediate, and terminal), you will work with compounding as a means of improving sentence structure through use of these three structures. Compounding adds one or more like phrases to a sentence.

Select one of your sentences containing an absolute phrase and add another absolute phrase. Do the same with the appositive and participle phrases. For example:

1d.   The handyman, **his tools randomly scattered over the workbench, his hands moving determinedly,** tried to make a little order out of the mess by putting all like things together. (*compound intermediate absolutes*)

2d.   After ruling out the cook, the baby-sitter, and the boy who cut their lawn, they decided that, with their unfortunate fallen financial state, they could only keep in their hire the handyman, **an elderly, neat gentleman with never a grease stain on his work clothes, a man in their employ for over two generations.** (*compound terminal appositives*)

3d.   The handyman, **painting over last year's paint on the old lawn furniture, acting upon his reputation as a perfectionist,** noticed a paint bubble, got out a straight pin, pricked it, scraped the loose paint away, then sanded it smooth. (*compound intermediate participles*)

Task Six

To review the three structures, the positions in which they may occur, and the methods by which they may be compounded, do the following. For each worker listed, write a sentence of at least twenty words describing the worker on the job. Include, underline, and punctuate the required phrase described in parentheses.

1.   BARTENDER (introductory absolute)
2.   JOCKEY (intermediate absolute)
3.   NEWSPAPER BOY (terminal absolute)
4.   BANK TELLER (introductory appositive)
5.   BABY–SITTER (intermediate appositive)
6.   FIREMAN (terminal appositive)
7.   ACTOR (introductory participle)
8.   MODEL (intermediate participle)
9.   TAXI DRIVER (terminal participle)
10. CHECKER AT A SUPERMARKET (introductory compound absolutes)
11. SECRETARY (intermediate compound absolutes)
12. TEACHER (terminal compound absolutes)
13. DANCER (introductory compound appositives)
14. WRITER (intermediate compound appositives)
15. TRUCK DRIVER (terminal compound appositives)
16. DETECTIVE (introductory compound participles)
17. SALESPERSON (intermediate compound participles)
18. WAITRESS (terminal compound participles)

19.　ARTIST (one of each—absolute, appositive, and participle—in any order, in any position)

PRACTICE 6

Now you will apply your knowledge of absolute, appositive, and participle phrases by writing paragraphs with sentences containing them. Write three separate paragraphs, unrelated to each other in content, describing three different workers on the job, "picturing" the worker for five or ten minutes as he or she performs the job. Although each of the three paragraphs asks you to use absolute, appositive, and participle phrases, the specific requirements for each paragraph are identified below.

Requirements for Paragraph One

1.　Paragraph must contain no more than five sentences.
2.　One sentence must contain an absolute in any position.
3.　One sentence must contain an appositive in any position.
4.　One sentence must contain a participle in any position.
5.　Punctuation of absolute, appositive, and participle phrases must be correct.
6.　Phrases (absolute, appositive, and participle) must be underlined. (Boldface type is used instead of underlining in the model below.)
7.　Phrases must be labeled.

For example:

The storekeeper, **a respected, self-reliant man with a balding head and a grey mustache,** (*appositive*) had had the ad in the newspaper for the past three weeks. **Standing on the ladder to put merchandise on the top shelf,** (*participle*) he heard the door open. A teen-aged boy stood near the cash register, and, seeing the owner, explained that he wanted to apply for the job as stock boy. The man climbed down the ladder, **his body moving slowly** (*absolute*). He needed the boy, he thought, and the boy needed him.

Requirements for Paragraph Two

1.　Paragraph must contain no more than five sentences.
2.　One sentence must contain compound absolutes in any position.
3.　One sentence must contain compound appositives in any position.
4.　One sentence must contain compound participles in any position.
5.　Punctuation of absolutes, appositives, and participles must be correct.

6. Phrases (absolute, appositive, and participle) must be underlined. (Boldface type is used instead of underlining in the model below.)
7. Phrases must be labeled.

For example:

His hands sweating from tension, his concentration focused, *(compound absolutes)* Sandy Marks walked to the mound. **Practicing his pitches until he felt total control, fixing the mound with precision to his satisfaction,** *(compound participles)* he planned the strategy. He checked the alignment of his players, then turned to face the first batter. After receiving the signal from the catcher, he wound up and threw a fastball, which the batter swung at but missed. The pitcher, **a rookie just brought up to the team, a showman with a dazzling style,** *(compound appositives)* strutted around the mound, the crowd roaring at each cocky move.

Requirements for Paragraph Three

1. Paragraph must contain no more than five sentences.
2. One sentence must contain an absolute, an appositive, and a participle in any order and in any position.
3. Punctuation must be correct.
4. Phrases must be underlined. (Boldface type is used instead of underlining in the model below.)
5. Phrases must be labeled.

For example:

Pushed to the brink of exhaustion there on the neon-lit dance floor, ego-fed by the hand-clapping crowd, they persisted, twirling, dipping, rhythmically moving to the stereo's obligato beat. The man, a dock worker in the daytime who spent every Friday night until closing time at Sweeney's, was the star of the dance floor, and he knew it. He counted on it, lived for it. With the girl beside him, more a foil than a partner, **a proficient dancer in whom his interest was strictly egotistical,** *(appositive)* they danced on, twenty minutes straight now non-stop, **her body like a top, his arms pulling her spinning toward him, then away,** *(absolute)* **moving his own body more furiously than hers, more desperately, making their illusory synchronization believable.** *(participle)* It was harder work than the docks.

PRACTICE 7

Expand the basic paragraph below by adding content to each sentence. Use at least two participles, three absolutes, and one appositive—in any order and in any position. Do not change any of the given content; only add to it. Make your expanded content different from the sample expansion shown.

Basic Paragraph

The soldier huddled in the trench. Enemy fire surrounded him. His best friend lay wounded beside him. A hand grenade exploded fifty yards away. He prayed.

Expansion

The soldier, a draftee two months off the farm, huddled in the trench, terrified that the company commander had just suffered a heart attack. Enemy fire surrounded him, bullets pinging off metal or thudding the ground, grenades exploding, voices shouting out the pain of injury. His best friend lay wounded beside him, thrashing and moaning from a shrapnel hit in the leg. A hand grenade exploded fifty yards away, debris showering the trench, blinding the troops huddled there. He prayed, eyes closed, hands clenched, all hope seemingly shattered.

Appositive

a draftee two months off the farm

Participles

terrified that the company commander had just suffered a heart attack (past participle)
thrashing and moaning from a shrapnel hit in the leg (present participles)
blinding the troops huddled there (present participle)

Absolutes

bullets pinging off metal or thudding the ground
grenades exploding
voices shouting out the pain of injury
debris showering the trench
eyes closed
hands clenched
all hope seemingly shattered

After you have finished this first paragraph, write another one using each of the structures (absolute, appositive, and participle phrases) at least once. The second paragraph should be a sequel to the first, and approximately the same length.

PRACTICE 8

The list of sentences below illustrates the use of a combination of these structures within a sentence. Using a combination is common in professional writing and worth incorporating judiciously into your own. First, for each sentence, identify the type of structure in boldface.

Short Sentences

1. **Gasping, his hands raw,** he reached a flat place at the top.
   Richard Connell, "The Most Dangerous Game"

2. He stood there, **his coat wet, holding his wet hat,** and said nothing.
   Ernest Hemingway, *A Farewell to Arms*

3. He stood quivering, **stiff ears forward, eyes rolling so that the whites showed, pretending to be frightened.**
   John Steinbeck, *The Red Pony*

4. He walked in the rain, **an old man with his hat off, a carabinieri on either side.**

   Ernest Hemingway, *A Farewell to Arms*

Medium Sentences

5. **One of many small groups of children, each child carrying his little bag of crackling,** we trod the long road home in the cold winter afternoon.
   Peter Abrahams, *Tell Freedom*

6. It ran, **its pelvic bones crushing aside trees and bushes, its taloned feet clawing damp earth, leaving prints six inches deep wherever it settled its weight.**

   Ray Bradbury, *A Sound of Thunder*

7. I turned to "Annabel Lee," and we walked up and down the garden rows, **the cool dirt between our toes, reciting the beautifully sad lines.**
   Maya Angelou, *I Know Why the Caged Bird Sings*

8. The masters were in their places for the first Chapel, **seated in stalls in front of and at right angles to us, suggesting by their worn expressions and careless postures that they had never been away at all.**
   John Knowles, *A Separate Peace*

Long Sentences

9. The midwife, **arriving late,** had found the baby's head pulled out of shape, **its neck stretched, its body warped**; and she had pushed the head back and molded the body with her hands.
   John Steinbeck, *Grapes of Wrath*

10. He trembled alone there in the middle of the park for hours, **wondering what would happen if he had an attack of appendicitis, unnerved by the**

thoughts of a fainting spell, horrified by the realization that he might have to move his bowels, until at last we came.

John Knowles, A Separate Peace

11.   Out in the distances the fans of windmills twinkled, **turning**, and about the base of each, about the drink tank, was a speckle of dark dots, **a gather of cattle grazing in moonlight and meditating upon good grass, block salt, impermanence, and love.**

Glendon Swarthout, Bless the Beasts and Children

12.   The day my son Laurie started kindergarten he renounced corduroy overalls with bibs and began wearing blue jeans with a belt; I watched him go off the first morning with the older girl next door, **seeing clearly that an era of my life was ended, my sweet-voiced nursery-school tot replaced by a long-trousered, swaggering character who forgot to stop at the corner and wave good-bye to me.**

Shirley Jackson, "Charles"

Next, write a paragraph in which you imitate the structures of three of the model sentences—one from the group of short sentences, one from the group of medium ones, and one from the group of long ones. In the rest of the sentences, aim for maturity of structure. For example:

1. Over by the meat counter the crowd of city women gathered, complaining, and amid the cluster of angry shoppers, amid the genuinely frustrated buyers, was a group of outspoken suburban ladies, delegates from Women's Outreach shouting in unison and calling for reduced prices, better grades of meat, wider assortment, and improved service. 2. One protester, Mrs. Cannon from Crestwood Valley, was uncomfortable, unaccustomed to mingling with suffering masses. 3 She stopped, her mind wondering about the ladies' motives and tactics, her confused conscience questioning her involvement there, demanding self-honesty whenever she tried rationalization. 4. The ladies were there not as consumer advocates, not as champions of the poor, she thought, but as graduates of assertiveness training, a dedicated group of self-improvers, not social reformers. 5. She walked away from the crowd, a realist among hypocrites, a disturbed look on her face.

The example paragraph succeeds because the student was able to make each sentence structurally mature, not just those based on model sentences. The imitations are successfully "hidden" in the paragraph. In your paragraph, do the same. Try to "hide" your three imitations so well that uncovering them would be difficult. (In the example paragraph, sentences 1, 3, and 5 are imitations of models 11, 6, and 4, respectively.)

The use of these three sentence parts is common in professional writing. The next Practices illustrate the frequency with which they occur. These Practices are all based on sentences from *A Separate Peace* by John Knowles, a study of the psychology of maturation in the lives of adolescent boys.

PRACTICE 9

Below are sentences that are reduced versions of John Knowles's original sentences, ones containing an absolute, appositive, or participle phrase. The phrases that have been deleted are listed underneath. Decide which phrase belongs with which reduced sentence. Identify the type of phrase—absolute, appositive, or participle. In order to do this, you will have to read each reduced sentence and each phrase carefully. Look for related meanings. After you finish the matching, write the complete sentence. If the phrase could be placed in more than one position within the sentence, write out the sentence more than once to reflect each possible effective placement.

Group One

1. You could by a prodigious effort jump far enough out into the river for safety.

2. He began scrambling up the wooden pegs nailed to the side of the tree.

3. Everyone shouted that Phineas must not be moved; someone else did not waste time going there but rushed to bring Dr. Stanpole from his house.

4. I washed the traces off me and then put on a pair of chocolate brown slacks and a blue flannel shirt.

5. Shoving in his long bamboo poles, he pushed deliberately forward and slid slowly away from me down the gradual slope as though to ward off any interference.

Phrases

A. his back muscles working like a panther's

B. a pair which Phineas had been particularly critical of when he wasn't wearing them

C. standing very upright, his skis far apart to guard against any threat to his balance, his poles sticking out on either side of him

D. realizing that only a night nurse would be at the Infirmary

E. standing on this limb

Group Two

6. He was sitting on his cot.

7. It was only that we could feel a deep and sincere difference between us and them.

8. He trembled alone there in the middle of the park for hours until at last we came.

9. The ocean was winter cold.

10. We left the party.

Phrases

A.   both of us feeling fine

B.   throwing up foaming sun-sprays across some nearby rocks

C.   wondering what would happen if he had an attack of appendicitis, unnerved by the thoughts of a fainting spell, horrified by the realization that he might have to move his bowels

D.   elbows on knees, looking down

E.   a difference which everyone struggled with awkward fortitude to bridge

Group Three

11.   We had dinner at a hot dog stand, with our backs to the ocean and its now cooler wind.

12.   To the right of them the gym meditated behind its gray walls.

13.   I took a step toward him, and then my knees bent, and I jounced the limb.

14.   After about ten minutes he came walking rapidly out of his office.

15.   The sun was the blessing of the morning.

Phrases

A.   our faces toward the heat of the cooking range

B.   his head down and his hands sunk in the pockets of his white smock

C.   the high, wide, oval-topped windows shining back at the sun

D.   holding firmly to the trunk

E.   the one celebrating element, an aesthete with no purpose except to shed radiance

Group Four

16.   The Devon faculty had never before experienced a student who combined a calm ignorance of the rules with a winning urge to be good, who seemed to love the school truly and deeply, and never more than when he was breaking the regulations.

17.   The tree was tremendous.

18.   I stood precariously in the middle of the room.

19.   The stadium itself, two white concrete banks of seats, was as powerful and alien to me as an Aztec ruin.

20.   The advance guard which came down the street from the railroad station consisted of a number of Jeeps.

Phrases

A. wanting desperately to leave and powerless to do so

B. being driven with a certain restraint, their gyration-prone wheels inactive on these old ways which offered nothing bumpier than a few cobblestones

C. a model boy who was most comfortable in the truant's corner

D. an irate, steely black steeple beside the river

E. filled with the traces of vanished people and vanished rites, of supreme emotions and supreme tragedies

Group Five

21. "What I like best about this tree," he said in that voice of his, "what I like is that it's such a cinch!"

22. Finny got up, patted my head genially, and moved on across the field.

23. The chocolate brown wicker furniture shot out menacing twigs, and three dozen of us stood tensely teetering our cups amid the wicker and leaves.

24. On this quiet old street, he looked like an invalid, house-bound.

25. In class he generally sat slouched in his chair.

Phrases

A. trying hard not to sound as inane in our conversation with the four present Masters and their wives as they sounded to us

B. not deigning to glance around for my counterattack, but relying on his extrasensory ears, his ability to feel in the air someone coming on him from behind

C. the equivalent in sound of a hypnotist's eyes

D. his alert face following the discussion with an expression of philosophical comprehension

E. propped now before a great New England fireplace

PRACTICE 10

The groups of sentences below are based on single sentences from *A Separate Peace* in which the author used an absolute, appositive, or participle phrase. Combine the sentences in each group into one sentence per group, using an absolute, an appositive, or a participle phrase.

Keep the first sentence in each group and add to it excerpts from the other sentence(s) in the group. The originals are in the References. Punctuate correctly.

1a. The ocean looked dead too.

b. Dead gray waves were hissing mordantly along the beach.

2a. We spent an odd day.

b. We were toiling in that railroad yard.

3a. I said nothing.

b. My mind was exploring the new dimensions of isolation around me.

4a. Others remembered that Phil Latham lived just across the Common and that he was an expert in first aid.

b. Phil Latham was the wrestling coach.

5a. There they all were now with their high I.Q.'s and expensive shoes, as Brinker had said, pasting each other with snowballs.

b. They were the cream of the school.

c. They were also the lights and leaders of the senior class.

6a. The masters were in their places for the first Chapel.

b. They were seated in stalls in front of and at right angles to us.

c. They were suggesting by their worn expressions and careless postures that they had never been away at all.

7a. His talk rolled on.

b. His talk was ignoring my look of shock and clumsiness.

c. His talk was also covering my look of shock and clumsiness.

8a. We reached the others loitering around the base of the tree, and Phineas began exuberantly to throw off his clothes.

b. Phineas was delighted by the fading glow of the day.

c. Phineas was delighted by the challenge of the tree.

d. Phineas was delighted by the competitive tension of all of us.

PRACTICE 11

Expand each reduced sentence below, using an absolute, an appositive, or a participle phrase of approximately the length indicated. When you finish, compare your work with the originals in the References.

1. Finny, /3 , swung his head around to look at me for an instant with extreme interest, and then he tumbled sideways, broke through the little branches below, and hit the bank with a sickening, unnatural thud. (absolute)

2. From my locker I collected my sneakers, jock strap, and gym pants, and then turned away, /8. (participle)

3.   It didn't seem fitting for Brinker Hadley, /5 , to be congratulating me on influence. (appositive)

4.   First there was the local apple crop, /15. (participle)

5.   With unthinking sureness I moved out on the limb and jumped into the river, /8. (absolute)

6.   The windows now had the closed blankness of night, a deadened look about them, /7 . (appositive)

7.   He came toward me, without his cane at the moment, /22 . (absolute)

8.   /6 , I could see with great clarity the fear I had lived in, which must mean that in the interval I had succeeded in a very important undertaking: I must have made my escape from it. (participle)

In the preceding Practices, you saw that the structures you are studying are used frequently by professional writers. Obviously, it's because of their great frequency that they are included in this textbook, where you can learn to use them in your own writing.

Not only is the use of these structures common in separate sentences of professional writers; it is also fairly common to find two or more of the same structures, or a combination of them, within the same sentence.

The following sentence* from *A Separate Peace* is the longest sentence in the book—approximately 120 words—a length uncommon even with professionals.

(1)   I thought of Phineas, not of the tree and pain,

(2)   but of one of his favorite tricks, Phineas in

(3)   exaltation, balancing on one foot on the prow of

(4)   a canoe like a river god, his raised arms invoking

(5)   the air to support him, face transfigured, body a

(6)   complex set of balances and compensations, each muscle

(7)   aligned in perfection with all the others to maintain

(8)   this supreme fantasy of achievement, his skin glowing

(9)   from immersions, his whole body hanging between

(10)   river and sky as though he had transcended gravity

(11)   and might by gently pushing upward with his foot

(12)   glide a little way higher and remain suspended

(13)   in space, encompassing all the glory of the summer

(14)   and offering it to the sky.

---

*Slightly adapted.

Notice that the entire sentence concerns the comparison of Phineas to a god (line 4). Phineas, one of the two main characters of *A Separate Peace*, one who is unique and special among all the characters in his escaping the fears common to the rest of the boys at his school, is in this sentence described in a way that emphasizes—through the sheer length and accumulation of descriptive detail—the uniqueness of this god-like character. The length of the sentence allows the reader to concentrate on that uniqueness and in so doing realize the emphatic difference between this boy and all the other boys on the campus.

The sentence, though extremely long, is tightly unified and organized. The unity is based on the generalization about Phineas stated in lines 2–3: *Phineas in exaltation*. The word *exaltation* means the state of being filled with pride, delight, elation—all of which apply to this god-like young man. The rest of the sentence, through citation of Phineas's almost supernatural physical and spiritual nature, supports the generalization concerning his exaltation and unifies the entire sentence. That unified image is conveyed through logical organization of the various sentence parts, each of which focuses on a part of Phineas's anatomy as he stands balancing on the prow of the canoe: his feet (line 3); his arms (line 4); his face (line 5); his body (line 5); his muscles (line 6); his skin (line 8); and finally, and appropriately placed at the end, his whole body (line 9). The organization of the sentence is brought to an emphatic end with the last sentence part, a participle phrase suggesting that Phineas, a young god acting like a priest in the worship of nature, performs a religious sacrifice: *encompassing all the glory of the summer and offering it to the sky.*

The structure of the sentence was obviously carefully planned. It is characterized mainly by the presence of participles and absolutes. They are arranged as follows: a participle phrase, then a series of absolute phrases, and at the end of the sentence another participle phrase. There is a symmetry in this arrangement that complements the organization of the sentence. It could be outlined as follows:

Central Image of Sentence (Phineas in Exaltation)

I. *Physical Action Conveying the Central Image*

balancing on one foot on the prow of a canoe like a river god, (*participle*)

II. *Indicators of the Central Image*

A. his raised arms invoking the air to support him, (*absolute*)

B. [his] face transfigured, (*absolute*)

C. [his] body a complex set of balances and compensations, (*absolute*)

D. each muscle aligned in perfection with all the others to maintain this supreme fantasy of achievement, (*absolute*)

E.   his skin glowing from immersions, (*absolute*)

F.   his whole body hanging between river and sky as though he had transcended gravity and might by gently pushing upward with his foot glide a little way higher and remain suspended in space, (*absolute*)

III. *Implication of the Central Image* (Priest)

encompassing all the glory of the summer and offering it to the sky. (*participle*)

PRACTICE 12

Even though a sentence of this length is uncommon, it would be good for you to practice imitating it. The sentence illustrates principles of sentence composing that apply to any well-written sentence, regardless of length: sentence unity, sentence organization, and the relation of both to special purposes intended by the writer.

Following the above outline, write an imitation of the sentence, aiming for strong unity and organization that relate to the central purpose. For example:

A.   I thought of Grandmom, not of her quick temper and constant complaining, but of the gracious way she entertained and treated guests in her home, Grandmom then in her glory, her hands skillfully preparing food, eyes sparkling as she watched the children playing, her feet scampering back and forth across her carefully-scrubbed kitchen floor, her mouth nonstop talking about her past, her combination of imagination and whimsy entrancing everyone, her spirit like that of a poet or a child, celebrating the family and smiling at the contentment her hospitality evoked.

B.   I thought of Chief, not of his emotions or mind, but of his bodily movement, Chief in frenzied command, looking down at the inmates from the third-story balcony of the yard, his arms waving like the sign language of a mute, head turning rapidly from side to side, lips in rapid movement, fingers pointing threateningly at men who weren't listening or paying attention, eyes searching the yard, his entire demeanor that of a frenzied bear, roaring out indecipherable sounds and stalking heavily about.

When you have finished your first draft, try outlining it in a way similar to the outline provided above for the model sentence. Your outline will reveal whether your sentence has the four essential ingredients for this—and every—well-written sentence: (1) central purpose, (2) unity, (3) logical organization, and (4) appropriate sentence structure. After you outline your sentence, you may need to revise it in order to give it these four ingredients.

PARAGRAPH EXPANDING

Paragraph expanding is an excellent way to apply to paragraphs the sentence composing techniques studied in *Sentence Composing 11*. The purpose of paragraph expanding is to approximate the act of writing: the composing of sentences that are integral parts of paragraphs. In the next series of Practices, you will form a partnership with a well-known author to produce a competent piece of writing. In each Practice, part of the author's original paragraph—usually one or two sentences—has been deleted. Using your best sentence composing ability, provide equivalent sentences for the deleted ones, following the directions provided.

In all paragraph expanding Practices, try to make your sentences every bit as good as the ones you are given by the author. Notice carefully the varied sentence structures, attention to detail, accuracy of word choice, and consistency of style; such writing qualities should guide and influence you as you write your sentences to add to the author's paragraph.

PRACTICE 13

Expand the paragraphs below by composing sentences that match the general description of the original sentences that have been deleted. Part of the description includes the suggested length for your sentence, based on the actual length of the deleted sentence.

Short: 1–15 words
Medium: 16–30 words
Long: 31–50 words

The second part of the description is the general topic, and the third part indicates the structure. Add sentences that will contribute to the paragraph's unity, organization, and consistency of style. When you finish, compare yours with the original in the References.

There is no way you can exactly duplicate the author's sentences, nor should you. The purpose of the Practice is to encourage you to approximate the quality of content and structure of the author's sentences, not to duplicate them. Consider yours acceptable if they meet the specified requirements and if they blend well with those of the author.

A.   From *A Separate Peace* by John Knowles, a paragraph narrating a swimmer breaking the school's record:

1.   We found a stop watch in the office.

2.   He mounted a starting box, leaned forward from the waist as he had seen racing swimmers do but never had occasion to do himself—I noticed a preparatory looseness coming into his shoulders and arms, a controlled ease about his stance which was unexpected in anyone trying to break a record.

3.   I said, "On your mark—Go!"

4.   There was a complex moment when his body uncoiled and shot forward with sudden metallic tension.

5.   *Length:* long, *Topic:* the swimmer completing the first lap, *Structure:* one highly modified absolute

6.   Another turn and up the pool again—I noticed no particular slackening of his pace—another turn, down the pool again, his hand touched the end, and he looked up at me with a composed, interested expression.

7.   "Well, how did I do?"

8.   I looked at the watch; he had broken A. Hopkins Parker's record by .7 second.

B.   From *Ethan Frome* by Edith Wharton, a paragraph describing a cat knocking over and breaking a valuable dish:

1.   The cat, unnoticed, had crept up on muffled paws from Zeena's seat to the table, and was stealthily elongating its body in the direction of the milk-jug, which stood between Ethan and Mattie.

2.   The two leaned forward at the same moment, and their hands met on the handle of the jug.

3.   Mattie's hand was underneath, and Ethan kept his clasped on it a moment longer than was necessary.

4.   *Length:* medium, *Topic:* the cat breaking the dish, *Structure:* one highly modified participle

C.   From *The Red Badge of Courage* by Stephen Crane, a paragraph describing a dead soldier:

1.   He was being looked at by a dead man who was seated with his back against a columnlike tree.

2.   The corpse was dressed in a uniform that once had been blue, but was now faded to a melancholy shade of green.

3.   *Length:* medium, *Topic:* the eyes of the corpse, *Structure:* one participle

4.   The mouth was open.

5.   Its red had changed to an appalling yellow.

6.   Over the gray skin of the face ran little ants.

7.   One was trundling some sort of a bundle along the lower lip.

D.   From *Call It Sleep* by Henry Roth, a paragraph describing a child spilling soup:

1.   He dared not refuse, though the very thought of eating sickened him.

2.   *Length:* medium, *Topic:* attempting to eat the first spoonful, *Structure:* one participle

3. Instead of reaching his mouth, the spoon reached only his chin, struck against the hollow under his lower lip, scalded it, fell from his nerveless fingers into the plate.

4. *Length:* short, *Topic:* soup splashing on his clothing and table cloth, *Structures:* series of two participles

5. With a feeling of terror David watched the crimson splotches on the cloth widen till they met each other.

E. From "All-Gold Cañon" by Jack London, a paragraph describing the shooting of a gold miner:

1. And while he debated, a loud, crashing noise burst on his ear.

2. At the same instant he received a stunning blow on the left side of the back, and from the point of impact felt a rush of flame through his flesh.

3. He sprang up in the air, but halfway to his feet collapsed.

4. *Length:* long, *Topic:* the miner falling to the ground, *Structures:* series of three absolutes

5. His legs twitched convulsively several times.

6. His body was shaken as with a mighty ague.

7. There was a slow expansion of the lungs, accompanied by a deep sigh.

8. Then the air was slowly, very slowly, exhaled, and his body as slowly flattened itself down into inertness.

F. From *Winesburg, Ohio* by Sherwood Anderson, a paragraph explaining an adolescent's philosophy of life:

1. There is a time in the life of every boy when he for the first time takes the backward view of life.

2. Perhaps that is the moment when he crosses the line into manhood.

3. The boy is walking through the street of his town.

4. He is thinking of the future and of the figure he will cut in the world.

5. Ambitions and regrets awake within him.

6. Suddenly something happens; he stops under a tree and waits as for a voice calling his name.

7. Ghosts of old things creep into his consciousness; the voices outside of himself whisper a message concerning the limitations of life.

8. From being quite sure of himself and his future he becomes not at all sure.

9. If he be an imaginative boy a door is torn open and for the first time he looks out upon the world, seeing, as though they marched in procession before him, the countless figures of men who before his time have come out of nothingness into the world, lived their lives and again disappeared into nothingness.

10. The sadness of sophistication has come to the boy.

11. With a little gasp he sees himself as merely a leaf blown by the wind through the streets of his village.

12. *Length:* long, *Topic:* the inevitability of death, *Structures:* series of two appositives

13. He shivers and looks eagerly about.

14. *Length:* medium, *Topic:* the shortness of life, *Structure:* one appositive

15. Already he hears death calling.

16. With all his heart he wants to come close to some other human, touch someone with his hands, be touched by the hand of another.

17. If he prefers that the other be a woman, that is because he believes that a woman will be gentle, that she will understand.

18. He wants, most of all, understanding.

References

INTRODUCTION

PRACTICE A (page 2)

In the middle of the room stood a big square table littered with playing cards, and around it were grouped boxes for the players to sit on.

PRACTICE B (page 3)

1. The horse had never been lustier, and it bolted its rider with abruptness, sharply stunning him from the suddenness, and galloped.

2. Stars twinkled on pieces of broken shells and on ruined sand castles in the sea-drenched sand of the beach that stretched miles, endless miles, its many shells strewn on it by high-crested waves.

PRACTICE C (page 4)

1. In the darkness in the hallway by the door, the sick woman arose and started again toward her own room.

2. Over the fire he stuck a wire grill, pushing the four legs down into the ground with his boot.

3. Near the edge of town, the group had to walk around an automobile burned and squatting on the narrow road, and the bearers on one side, unable to see their way in the darkness, fell into a deep ditch.

PRACTICE D (page 5)

1. Like many Southern Black children, he lived with his grandmother, who was as strict as Momma and as kind as she knew how to be.

2. Sitting down at her desk, she wrote a short note to Mrs. Harvey, in which she briefly outlined her reasons for going.

PUNCTUATION AND SENTENCE COMPOSING

PRACTICE 1 (pages 8–9)

Note: Accept a variation from these sentence structures as long as punctuation marks are correctly placed and the sentence is logically organized.

1. A few stray white bread crumbs lay on the cleanly washed floor by the table; putting the lamp upon a low stool, he began to pick up the crumbs, carrying them to his mouth one by one with unbelievable rapidity.

2. A tall, shambling dark young fellow, whom Dr. Schumann remembered as having embarked at some port in Texas, had gone ashore and was now returning; he lounged along in the wake of the Spanish girls, regarding them with what could only be described as a leer.

3. He has always wished they were on the eastern side of the building, preferring to look out on frozen cliffs of water in winter, rather than dirty streets, dirtier cars; it is not a pleasant corner in the midst of the gray Chicago winter.

4. For a moment Augustus thought of throwing himself in the way of the horses to stop them, but before the carriage reached him, something gave way; first one and then the other of the horses detached itself from the carriage and came galloping past him.

PRACTICE 2 (page 10)

1. He came to the corner of the rock and paused, sank until his belly softly scraped the sand, and became one with the bottom's shadows; **then, sinuous as a snake, he began to flow around the rock.**

2. The new liner was 66,000 tons displacement; **Robertson's was 70,000 tons.** The real ship was 882.5 feet long; **the fictional one was 800 feet.**

3. **Dr. Phillips threw off his leather coat and built a fire in the tin stove**; he set a kettle of water on the stove and dropped a can of beans into the water.

4. **The day my son Laurie started kindergarten he renounced corduroy overalls with bibs and began wearing blue jeans with a belt**; I watched him go off the first morning with the older girl next door, seeing clearly that an era of my life was ended, my sweet-voiced nursery-school tot replaced by a long-trousered swaggering character who forgot to stop at the corner and wave good-bye to me.

PRACTICE 3 (page 11)

1. If you walk through the museums of the world, you will find a variety of instruments of torture: racks, thumbscrews, barbed whips, iron maidens, pincers, branding irons, machines for electric shock.
List. Not like a sentence.

2. He borrowed seed, sowed the land he had bought: it produced well.
Explanation. Like a sentence.

3. At the latest possible moment, a bridal party appeared in a festival flurry at the foot of the gangplank: a profusion of lace hats and tender-colored gauzy frocks for the women, immaculate white linen and carnation buttonholes for the men.
List. Not like a sentence.

4. The narrow creek was like a ditch: tortuous, fabulously deep, filled with gloom under the thin strip of pure and shining blue of the heaven.
Explanation and description. Not like a sentence.

PRACTICE 4 (pages 12–13)

Note: Accept a variation from these sentence structures as long as punctuation marks are correctly placed and the sentence is logically organized.

1. But whether he was being brilliant or dull, he had one sole topic of conversation: himself.

2. He has caught her off-guard, but she is still more poised than he, and this close he can see her face: small, delicate features, the casual elegance of a painter or a dancer, a beautiful pointed nose.

3. But his real history is much longer and much more extraordinary than could be indicated by these flares of war: it is history that runs back three centuries into primitive America, a strange and unfathomable history that is touched by something dark and supernatural.

4. I recalled only a few cracked relics from slavery times: an iron pot, an ancient bell, a set of ankle-irons and links of chain, a primitive loom, a spinning wheel, a gourd for drinking, an ugly ebony African god that seemed to sneer (presented to the school by some traveling millionaire), a leather whip with copper brads, a branding iron with the double letter *IV M.*

PRACTICE 5 (pages 13–14)

1. He could never escape them, no matter how much or how far he ran: **a man going on sixty could not run that far.**

2. Under the ceaseless conflagration of lightning that flamed in the skies, everything below stood out in clear-cut and shadowless distinctness: **the bending trees, the billowy river, white with foam, the driving spray of spume flakes, the dim outlines of the high bluffs on the other side, glimpsed through the drifting cloudwrack and the slanting veil of rain.**

3. They began to ransack the floor: **pulled beds away from walls, tore clothes off hooks in the closets, pulled suitcases and boxes off shelves.**

4.   Your friends are all the dullest dogs I know. They are not beautiful: **they are only decorated**. They are not clean: **they are only shaved and starched**. They are not dignified: **they are only fashionably dressed**. They are not educated: **they are only college passmen**. They are not religious: **they are only pewrenters**. They are not moral: **they are only conventional**.

PRACTICE 6 (pages 14–15)

1.   In two respects it was an exceptionally safe car: first, it didn't go very fast; second, it had three foot pedals. . . .

2.   There were all the human smells too of the hundreds of people who filled the boardwalk: ladies in print dresses smelling like passing gardens; swimmers with their scents of sun-tan oils and skin lotions. . . .

3.   *The Martian Chronicles* makes use of a dozen or more stock ingredients of pulp science-fiction: mental telepathy, materialized fantasies, robots, mass hypnosis, intersecting time-planes, super-creatures made of blue phosphorous light. . . .

4.   The little flotilla then set out across the uncharted San Francisco Bay: Sutter, with his title of captain which he had invented in the same manner that he had conjured up his role of empire builder; the eight Kanaka men and two Kanaka women who had contracted to stay with him for three years and help build his settlement; a fourteen-year-old Indian boy whom he had bought for $100 in the Wind River Rendezvous; a German cabinetmaker; three recruits from Yerba Buena; and several sailors on the beach.

5.   We hold these truths to be self-evident: that all men are created equal; that they are endowed by their Creator with certain inalienable rights; that among these are life, liberty, and the pursuit of happiness; that to secure these rights, governments are instituted among men, deriving their just powers from the consent of the governed; that whenever any form of government becomes destructive of these ends, it is the right of the people to alter or abolish it, and to institute a new government, laying its foundation on such principles, and organizing its powers in such form, as to them shall seem most likely to effect their safety and happiness.

PRACTICE 7 (pages 15–16)

1.   (A) – colon
    (B) – comma
    (C) – comma

2.   (A) – colon
    (B) – comma
    (C) – semicolon
    (D) – comma

3.   (A) – semicolon
      (B) – colon

4.   (A) – colon
      (B) – comma

5.   (A) – colon
      (B) – comma
      (C) – comma
      (D) – comma
      (E) – comma

6.   (A) – colon
      (B) – comma
      (C) – comma

7.   (A) – colon

8.   (A) – colon
      (B) – comma
      (C) – comma
      (D) – semicolon
      (E) – comma
      (F) – comma
      (G) – semicolon
      (H) – comma
      (I) – semicolon
      (J) – comma
      (K) – comma
      (L) – comma

PRACTICE 9 (pages 17–18)

1.   Over the table, where a collection of cloth samples was scattered—Samsa was a commercial traveler—hung the picture that he had recently cut from an illustrated paper and had put in a pretty gilded frame.

2.   The one permanent emotion of the inferior man, as of all simpler mammals, is fear—fear of the unknown, the complex, the inexplicable.

3.   And a man of exactly my own age—or perhaps he was a little older—got up and offered me his seat.

4.   Each is a cusp projecting seaward; between each pair of capes the beach runs in a long curving arc—the expression of the rhythmically swirling waters of the Gulf Stream eddies.

PRACTICE 10 (page 18)

1.   At first he thought the men all looked alike—**weathered cheeks, blue or black shirts, faded pants**—and then he saw the man with the yellow eyes.

2.   Compared with this gridwork, the natural landscape—**flat here, a little rolling there, a river valley, a pond**—just can't quite catch your attention.

3.   When Gregor had half his body out of bed—**the new method seemed more like a game than a task, for he had only to swing himself on his back**—he began to think how easily he could have got up if only he had had a little assistance.

4.   You want to be head of the class, valedictorian, so you can make a speech on Graduation Day—**in Latin or something boring like that probably**—and be the boy wonder of the school.

PRACTICE 12 (pages 19–20)

1.   The article was a furious denunciation of Mencken, concluding with one hot, short sentence: Mencken is a fool.

2.   It was a great luxury: eating what you wanted, sleeping all day if you wanted.

3.   For her pallbearers only her friends were chosen: her Latin teacher, W. L. Holtz; her high school principal, Rice Brown; her doctor, Frank Foncannon; her friend, W. H. Finney; her pal at the "Gazette" office, Walter Hughes; and her brother Bill.

4.   It was not only money that mattered: there were also strength, beauty, charm, athleticism, and something called "guts" or "character," which in reality meant the power to impose your will on others.

5.   He was not only the most important person in the world, to himself; in his own eyes he was the only person who existed.

6.   It is rather for us to be here dedicated to the great task remaining before us—that from these honored dead we take increased devotion to that cause for which they gave the last full measure of devotion; that we here highly resolve that these dead shall not have died in vain; that this nation, under God, shall have a new birth of freedom; and that government of the people, by the people, and for the people, shall not perish from the earth.

7.   It is really one of the odd sights of the world, and it is strictly an air sight: a whole country laid out in a mathematical gridwork, in sections one mile square each; exact, straight-sided, lined up in endless lanes that run precisely—and I mean precisely—North–South and East–West.

SENTENCE COMPOSING WITH ABSOLUTE PHRASES

PRACTICE 1 (pages 23–24)

1.   High in the air, a little figure, **his hands thrust in his short jacket pockets,** stood staring out to sea. (S-V split)

2.   He walked with a prim strut, swinging out his legs in a half-circle with each step, **his heels biting smartly into the red velvet carpet on the floor.** (sentence closer)

3.   Outside, **his carpetbag in his hand,** he stood for a time in the barnyard. (sentence opener)

4.   Freddy Malins clambered in after her and spent a long time settling her on the seat, **Mr. Browne helping him with advice.** (sentence closer, with no possessive pronoun at the beginning)

5.   Father lay crumped up on the stone floor of the pantry, [his] face down, [his] arms twisted at a curious angle. . . . (sentence closers, with the possessive pronoun *his* implied in each)

PRACTICE 2 (pages 25–26)

1. The author uses the intermediate position.

Introductory Position (acceptable)

Its amusements a mere glimmer of Palisades or Coney Island, the park, formal, unlovely, had already disappointed him.

Intermediate Position (acceptable)

The park, formal, unlovely, **its amusements a mere glimmer of Palisades or Coney Island,** had already disappointed him.

Terminal Position (acceptable)

The park, formal, unlovely, had already disappointed him, **its amusements a mere glimmer of Palisades or Coney Island.**

2. The author uses the terminal position.

Introductory Position (unacceptable)

The moonlight on her face, I was awake for quite a long time, thinking about things and watching Catherine sleeping.

Intermediate Position (unacceptable)

I, **the moonlight on her face,** was awake for quite a long time, thinking about things and watching Catherine sleeping.

Terminal Position (acceptable)

I was awake for quite a long time, thinking about things and watching Catherine sleeping, **the moonlight on her face.**

3. The author uses the introductory position, following the use of an introductory appositive phrase.

Introductory Position (acceptable)

One of many small groups of children, **each child carrying his little bag of crackling,** we trod the long road home in the cold winter afternoon.

Intermediate Position (unacceptable)

One of many small groups of children, we, **each child carrying his little bag of crackling,** trod the long road home in the cold winter afternoon.

Terminal Position (acceptable)

One of many small groups of children, we trod the long road home in the cold winter afternoon, **each child carrying his little bag of crackling.**

4. The author uses the terminal position.

Introductory Position (unacceptable)

Each set upon a carved wooden base, I looked across to a lighted case of Chinese design which held delicate-looking statues of horses and birds, small vases and bowls.

Intermediate Position (unacceptable)

I, **each set upon a carved wooden base,** looked across to a lighted case of Chinese design which held delicate-looking statues of horses and birds, small vases and bowls.

Terminal Position (acceptable)

I looked across to a lighted case of Chinese design which held delicate-looking statues of horses and birds, small vases and bowls, **each set upon a carved wooden base.**

PRACTICE 3 (pages 26–28)

1.   Then the rope tightened mercilessly while Buck struggled in fury, **his tongue lolling out of his mouth** and **his great chest panting.**

2.   It ran, **its pelvic bones crushing aside trees and bushes, its taloned feet clawing damp earth,** leaving prints six inches deep wherever it settled its weight.

3.   She was now standing arms akimbo, **her shoulders drooping a little, her head cocked to one side, her glasses winking in the sunlight.**

4.   And then, **his feet sinking in the soft nap of the carpet, his hand in one pocket clutching the money,** he felt as if he could squeal or laugh out loud.

5.   Within, you could hear the signs and murmurs as the furthest chambers of it died, **the organs malfunctioning, liquids running a final instant from pocket to sac to spleen, everything shutting off,** closing up forever.

6.   Just behind him a tall boy with glittering golden hair and a sulky mouth pushed and jostled a light wheel chair along, in which sat a small weary dying man with weak dark whiskers flecked with gray, **his spread hands limp on the brown rug over his knees, eyes closed.**

7.   We had long thought of them as a tableau, **Miss Emily a slender figure in white in the background, her father a spraddled silhouette in the foreground, his back to her** and clutching a horsewhip, **the two of them framed by the back-flung front door.**

PRACTICE 4 (pages 28–29)

1.   A fermile with a pencil grooged down and blatted nignly toward a wind-swept stapler, its back teeth slamting and gorgling the steamed brick under the oven.

2.   One customer in the line spoke out and ranted continuously about the unfair price, the other customers rallying and demanding the same reduction in the cost.

3.   Several dancers near the band joined together and moved quickly into two lines, one couple heading and leading the rest through the complicated steps.

PRACTICE 5 (page 29)

First Sentence Part

Model: The motorcycle on the sidewalk speeded up
First Imitation: A fermile with a pencil grooged down
Second Imitation: One customer in the line spoke out
Third Imitation: Several dancers near the band joined together

Second Sentence Part

Model: and skidded obliquely
First Imitation: and blatted nignly
Second Imitation: and ranted continuously
Third Imitation: and moved quickly

Third Sentence Part

Model: into a plate-glass window,
First Imitation: toward a wind-swept stapler,
Second Imitation: about the unfair price,
Third Imitation: into two lines,

Fourth Sentence Part (Absolute Phrase)

Model: the front wheel bucking and climbing the brick base beneath the window.
First Imitation: its back teeth slamting and gorgling the steamed brick under the oven.
Second Imitation: the other customers rallying and demanding the same reduction in cost.
Third Imitation: one couple heading and leading the rest through the complicated steps.

PRACTICE 6 (pages 30–31)

1. B
2. C
3. A

PRACTICE 7 (page 31)

1. This sentence matches model #2 in Practice 6.
2. This sentence matches model #1 in Practice 6.
3. This sentence matches model #3 in Practice 6.

PRACTICE 9 (pages 32–33)

1. The town lay on a broad estuary, **its old yellow plastered buildings hugging the beach**.
2. Like giants they toiled, **days flashing on the heels of days like dreams as they heaped the treasure up**.
3. In solid phalanxes the leaders crowded about the three jaguars, **tusks thrust forward, their little eyes bloodshot with anger and with battle lust**.

4.   An Arab on a motorcycle, **his long robes flying in the wind of his speed,** passed John at such a clip that the spirals of dust from his turnings on the winding road looked like little tornadoes.

PRACTICE 10 (pages 33–36)

A.   The youngest brother was nearby resting, **all his work over.**

B.   As soon as it was over, they pranced around Gracie like courtiers, **Paul wooing her disgustingly with his stretched smiles.**

C.   Later, somewhat sorry, he held the baby soothingly, and brought the music box to her and wound the toy up, **his voice singing with it.**

D.   The student teacher erased everything quickly and, with a hurried cover-up, started to call out the spelling words for us, **her embarrassment definitely coming from her misspelling on the chalkboard.**

PRACTICE 11 (pages 36–37)

1.   I could hear him crashing down the hill toward the sea, **the frightening laughter echoing back.**

2.   Finny and I went along the Boardwalk in our sneakers and white slacks, **Finny in a light blue polo shirt** and **I in a T-shirt.**

3.   And all the time he was reading the newspaper, his wife, a fat woman with a white face, leaned out of the window, gazing into the street, **her thick white arms folded under her loose breast on the window sill.**

4.   To the right of them the gym meditated behind its gray walls, **the high, wide, oval-topped windows shining back at the sun.**

PRACTICE 12 (pages 37–38)

1.   He began scrambling up the wooden pegs nailed to the side of the tree, **his back muscles working like a panther's.**

2.   They were smiling, **one woman talking, the others listening.**

3.   Touser roused himself under Fowler's desk and scratched another flea, **his leg thumping hard against the floor.**

4.   Men, **their caps pulled down, their collars turned up,** swung by; a few women all muffled scurried along; and one tiny boy, **only his little black arms and legs showing out of a white wooly shawl,** was jerked along angrily between his father and mother; he looked like a baby fly that had fallen into the cream.

PRACTICE 13 (pages 38–39)

1.   His great chest was low to the ground, **his head forward and down, his feet flying like mad, the claws scarring the hard-packed snow in parallel grooves.**

2.   Now, in the waning daylight, he turned into Glover Street toward his home, **his arms swinging as he moved onto the unpaved road.**

3.   As they drove off Wilson saw her standing under the big tree, looking pretty rather than beautiful in her faintly rosy khaki, **her dark hair drawn back off her forehead and gathered in a knot low on her neck, her face as fresh, he thought, as though she were in England.**

4.   In front of the house where we lived, the mountain went down steeply to the little plain along the lake, and we sat on the porch of the house in the sun and saw the winding of the road down the mountain-side and the terraced vineyards on the side of the lower mountain, **the vines all dead now for the winter** and **the fields divided by stone walls,** and below the vineyards, **the houses of the town on the narrow plain along the lake shore.**

SENTENCE COMPOSING
WITH APPOSITIVE PHRASES

PRACTICE 1 (page 42)

The appositive word is capitalized, and the appositive phrase is in boldface and correctly punctuated. Underlining indicates the word that the appositive phrase identifies.

1.   The face of Liliana Methold, **the fifth WOMAN in the plane,** was badly bruised and covered with blood. (S-V split)

2.   One of these dogs, **the best ONE,** had disappeared. (S-V split)

3.   Mr. Mick Malloy, **CASHIER at the Ulster and Connaught Bank,** draped his grey sports jacket neatly on a hanger and put on his black shantung work coat. (S-V split)

4.   **A self-educated MAN,** he had accepted the necessary smattering facts of science with a serene indulgence, as simply so much further proof of what the Creator could do when He put His hand to it. (sentence opener)

5.   Halfway there he heard the sound he dreaded, **the hollow, rasping COUGH of a horse.** (sentence closer)

6.   The writer, **an old MAN with a white mustache,** had some difficulty in getting into bed. (S-V split)

7.   In our clenched fists we held our working cards from the shop, **those sacred CARDS that we thought meant security.** (sentence closer)

PRACTICE 2 (pages 44–45)

1. *Introductory Position* (acceptable)

A fragile-faced beauty not yet ten years old, she sat demurely, her blonde hair flowing down her back.

Intermediate Position (acceptable)

She, **a fragile-faced beauty not yet ten years old**, sat demurely, her blonde hair flowing down her back.

Terminal Position (acceptable)

Her blonde hair flowing down her back, she sat demurely, **a fragile-faced beauty not yet ten years old**.

2. *Introductory Position* (acceptable)

A twelve year old daredevil rider, Rosemary hung up her spurs, tired from the long ride.

Intermediate Position (acceptable)

Rosemary, **a twelve year old daredevil rider**, hung up her spurs, tired from the long ride.

Terminal Position (unacceptable)

Rosemary hung up her spurs, tired from the long ride, **a twelve year old daredevil rider**.

3. *Introductory Position* (acceptable)

The star gymnast who captured the world with her performance, Nadia smiled softly at the ineptitude of her competitors.

Intermediate Position (acceptable)

Nadia, **the star gymnast who captured the world with her performance**, smiled softly at the ineptitude of her competitors.

Terminal Position (unacceptable)

Nadia smiled softly at the ineptitude of her competitors, **the star gymnast who captured the world with her performance**.

4. *Introductory Position* (acceptable)

The king of rock and roll and the subject of controversy, Elvis Presley left behind millions of bereaved fans.

Intermediate Position (acceptable)

Elvis Presley, **the king of rock and roll and the subject of controversy**, left behind millions of bereaved fans.

Terminal Position (unacceptable)

Elvis Presley left behind millions of bereaved fans, **the king of rock and roll and the subject of controversy.**

PRACTICE 3 (pages 45–46)

1. One of them, **a slender young man with white hands, the son of a jeweler in Winesburg,** talked continually of virginity.
2. In the late afternoon Will Henderson, **owner and editor of the *Eagle*,** went over to Tom Willy's saloon.
3. Buck stood and looked on, **the successful champion, the dominant primordial beast who had made his kill and found it good.**
4. Mr. Mick Malloy, **tall, young secret gambler with devil-may-care eyes and a long humorous nose,** became Mr. Malloy, **tall cashier with a dignified face, a gentlemanly bank clerk, a nice sort of fellow.**
5. Everything necessary, **books, music, wine,** he could receive in any quantity by sending a note through the window.

PRACTICE 4 (page 47)

1. Near the croop the big stonnert ladled, froopy and pasty and tumeous, **the blurt and the temician of the beach.** (Appositive phrase identifies "stonnert.")
2. By the podium scholarly Henrietta stood, intelligent and composed and smiling, **president and valedictorian of the senior class.** (Appositive phrase identifies "Henrietta.")
3. Under the canopy they danced, beaming and affectionate and happy, **the bride and groom in their finery.** (Appositive phrase identifies "they.")

PRACTICE 5 (page 48)

First Sentence Part

Model: Beside the fireplace
First Imitation: Near the croop
Second Imitation: By the podium
Third Imitation: Under the canopy

Second Sentence Part

Model: Old Doctor Winter sat,
First Imitation: the big stonnert ladled,
Second Imitation: scholarly Henrietta stood,
Third Imitation: they danced,

Third Sentence Part

Model: bearded and simple and benign,
First Imitation: froopy and pasty and tumeous,
Second Imitation: intelligent and composed and smiling,
Third Imitation: beaming and affectionate and happy,

Fourth Sentence Part (Appositive Phrase)

Model: historian and physician to the town.
First Imitation: the blurt and the temician of the beach.
Second Imitation: president and valedictorian of the senior class.
Third Imitation: the bride and groom in their finery.

PRACTICE 6 (pages 48–49)

1.   B
2.   C
3.   B

PRACTICE 7 (pages 49–50)

1.   This sentence matches model #1 in Practice 6.
2.   This sentence matches model #3 in Practice 6.
3.   This sentence matches model #2 in Practice 6.

PRACTICE 9 (pages 51–52)

1.   On this Sunday morning the postman and the policeman had gone fishing in the boat of Mr. Corell, **the popular store-keeper.**

2.   The real estate agent, **an old man with a smiling, hypocritical face,** soon joined them.

3.   They approached the domed synagogue with its iron weathercock, **a pock-marked yellow-walled building with an oak door,** for the time being resting in peace.

4.   Lieutenant Tonder was a poet, **a bitter poet who dreamed of perfect, ideal love of elevated young men for poor girls.**

5.   Out of the flaming wreckage was born another of the legends surrounding the Stanley Steamer, **the best car of its era but also the most misunderstood and maligned.**

PRACTICE 10 (pages 52–55)

A.   Near the statue was an obvious tourist, **an oriental lady with a Kodak camera.**

B.   *Gone with the Wind,* **the movie with the most re-issues,** originated as a novel of the old South by an un-glamorous and unknown authoress.

C.   "Missouri" is a special casserole, **a blend of potatoes and stewed tomatoes and hamburger.**

D.   We were far from our destination and were making good time on the interstate, but no time to squander, and Dad wouldn't stop more than twice a day although we kids were itchy, and Mom, **a shrewd, gentle arbitrator with Solomon's mind,** circumvented some flare-ups, and those she couldn't she left to Heaven.

PRACTICE 11 (pages 55–56)

1.   At the gate, I show the pass to a young Japanese private, **the sentry.**

2.   When he was twelve, his mother married an executive of a machine tool company in Cleveland, **an engineer who had adult children of his own.**

3.   **A modern intelligent woman,** my patient with her five children seemed in many ways as trapped as her forebears in Victorian times before the emancipation of women. . . .

4.   On the bark of the tree was scored the name of Deacon Peabody, **an eminent man,** who had waxed wealthy by driving shrewd bargains with the Indians.

PRACTICE 12 (page 57)

1.   He, **the enlightened man who looks afar in the dark,** had fled because of his superior perceptions and knowledge.

2.   There was Major Hunter, **a haunted little man of figures, a little man who, being a dependable unit, considered all other men either as dependable units or as unfit to live.**

3.   My bed was an army cot, **one of those affairs which are made wide enough to sleep on comfortably only by putting up, flat with the middle section, the two sides which ordinarily hang down like the sideboards of a drop-leaf table.**

4.   I had hardly any patience with the serious work of life which, not that it stood between me and desire, seemed to me child's play, **ugly monotonous child's play.**

PRACTICE 13 (pages 58–59)

1.   Perhaps two or three times a year we would come together at a party, one of those teen-age affairs which last until dawn with singing and dancing and silly games such as "Kiss the Pillow," or "Post Office," **the game which permits one to call for the creature of one's choice and embrace her furtively in a dark room.**

2.   Thus, one noontime, coming back from the office lunch downstairs a little earlier than usual, he found her and several of the foreign-family girls, as well as four of the American girls, surrounding Polish Mary, **one of the gayest and roughest of the foreign-family girls,** who was explaining in rather a high key how a certain "feller" whom she had met the night before had given her a beaded bag, and for what purpose.

3.   The rest were standing around in hatless, smoky little groups of twos and threes and fours inside the heated waiting room, talking in voices that, almost without exception, sounded collegiately dogmatic, as though each young man, in his strident, conversational turn, was clearing up, once and for all, some highly controversial issue, **one that the outside, non-matriculating world had been bungling, provocatively or not, for centuries.**

4.   Out in the distances the fans of windmills twinkled, turning, and about the base of each, about the drink tank, was a speckle of dark dots, **a gather of cattle grazing in moonlight and meditating upon good grass, block salt, impermanence, and love.**

SENTENCE COMPOSING
WITH PARTICIPLE PHRASES

PRACTICE 1 (pages 65–66)

1.   participle phrase
Away she darted. (sentence)

2.   verb phrase
The Fog Horn, once every fifteen seconds (non-sentence)

3.   participle phrase
Some taller buildings push up out of the feathery plain, like the fur hood Ma wears, only whiter. (sentence)

4.   participle phrase
The huge eye on the right side of its anguished head glittered before me like a caldron, into which I might drop. (sentence)

5.   participle phrase
Through days of torment he endlessly struggled not to love her; he escaped it. (sentence)

6.   verb phrase
The old banker, recalling to his mind the party he gave in the autumn fifteen years before. (non-sentence)

participle phrase
The old banker was pacing from corner to corner of his study. (sentence)

PRACTICE 2 (pages 67–68)

1b. unacceptable
1c. unacceptable

2b. acceptable
2c. unacceptable
2d. unacceptable

3b. unacceptable
3c. acceptable
3d. unacceptable

4b. unacceptable
4c. acceptable
4d. unacceptable

PRACTICE 5 (page 71)

1. **Being occupied with the misfortune the little round balls had wrought within him,** the bear gave him no notice. (present, sentence opener)

2. Manuel, **lying on the ground,** kicked at the bull's muzzle with his slippered feet. (present, S-V split)

3. **Clutching the clawing kitten to her collarbone,** her hair in her open mouth, she bawled encouragement to them. (present, sentence opener)

4. They were diggers in clay, **transformed by lantern light into a race of giants.** (past, sentence closer)

5. Ruthie, **dressed in a real dress of pink muslin that came below her knees,** was a little serious in her young-ladiness. (past, S-V split)

6. A little girl marched, **stepping neatly over arms and legs she did not look at.** (present, sentence closer)

7. **Swinging their grocery bags full of clean watery green onions and odorous liverwurst and red catsup and white bread,** they would dare each other on past the limits set by their stern mothers. (present, sentence opener)

8. Sometimes a gaggle of them came to the Store, **filling the whole room, chasing out the air,** and **even changing the well-known scents.** (present, sentence closer; present, sentence closer; present, sentence closer)

PRACTICE 6 (pages 72–73)

1. The author uses the intermediate position.

Introductory Position (acceptable)

Wearing a black turtleneck sweater, dirty flannels, and slippers, Bernard was waiting on the landing outside.

Intermediate Position (acceptable)

Bernard, **wearing a black turtleneck sweater, dirty flannels, and slippers,** was waiting on the landing outside.

Terminal Position (acceptable)

Bernard was waiting on the landing outside, **wearing a black turtleneck sweater, dirty flannels, and slippers.**

2. The author uses the introductory position.

Introductory Position (acceptable)

Sitting up in bed eating breakfast, we could see the lake and the mountains across the lake on the French side.

Intermediate Position (acceptable)

We, **sitting up in bed eating breakfast,** could see the lake and the mountains across the lake on the French side.

Terminal Position (unacceptable)

We could see the lake and the mountains across the lake on the French side, **sitting up in bed eating breakfast.**

3. The author uses the introductory position.

Introductory Position (acceptable)

Coming down the pole, I had a sense of being whirled violently through the air, with no control over my movements.

Intermediate Position (acceptable)

I, **coming down the pole,** had a sense of being whirled violently through the air, with no control over my movements.

Terminal Position (unacceptable)

I had a sense of being whirled violently through the air, with no control over my movements, **coming down the pole.**

4. The author uses the intermediate position.

Introductory Position (acceptable)

Perched on high piles, a little house appeared black in the distance.

Intermediate Position (acceptable)

A little house, **perched on high piles,** appeared black in the distance.

Terminal Position (unacceptable)

A little house appeared black in the distance, **perched on high piles.**

5. The author uses the terminal position.

Introductory Position (unacceptable)

When we had made our way downstairs, **screaming and begging to be allowed to go with her mother,** we saw the woman with the lovely complexion, Miss Pilzer.

Intermediate Position (unacceptable)

When we had made our way downstairs, we, **screaming and begging to be allowed to go with her mother,** saw the woman with the lovely complexion, Miss Pilzer.

Terminal Position (acceptable)

When we had made our way downstairs, we saw the woman with the lovely complexion, Miss Pilzer, **screaming and begging to be allowed to go with her mother.**

PRACTICE 7 (pages 73–74)

1.   He was a blind beggar, **carrying the traditional battered cane** and **thumping his way before him with the cautious, half-furtive effort of the sightless.**

2.   The passengers, **emerging from the mildewed dimness of the customs sheds, blinking their eyes against the blinding sunlight,** all had the look of invalids crawling into the hospital on their last legs.

3.   And so we went to the station, across the meadow, **taking the longer way, trying to be together as long as possible**.

4.   That winter my mother and brother came, and we set up housekeeping, **buying furniture on the installment plan, being cheated**, and yet **knowing no way to avoid it**.

5.   Instead of sleeping that night, we pored over the schematic diagram of her structures, **tracing the thoughts through mazes of her wiring, severing the leaders, implanting heterones**, as Dave called them.

6.   **Jumping to his feet** and **breaking off the tale**, Doctor Parcival began to walk up and down in the office of the *Winesburg Eagle*, where George Willard sat listening.

7.   A young Mexican woman, **softened and dispirited by recent childbirth, dressed in the elegant, perpetual mourning of her caste**, came up slowly, **leaning on the arm of the Indian nurse who carried her baby**, his long embroidered robe streaming over her arm almost to the ground.

8.   **Tugged here and there in his stockinged feet, bewildered by the numbers, staggered by so much raw flesh**, Dr. Sasaki lost all sense of profession and stopped working as a skillful surgeon and a sympathetic man; he became an automaton, **mechanically wiping, daubing, winding, wiping, daubing, winding**.

PRACTICE 8 (pages 75–76)

1.   When they fusted nearby in a zurner, he confrusticated about his nestings and purted about them, smiling and turling stews and red bleeps of wrinkled networks to the morm who flurded and narred cranster and cranster over the frame.

2.   As her arm whirled fast over the egg-whites, her face shifted toward the cookbook and stared at it, grimacing and expressing confusion and frustration over the third direction in the recipe that listed and explained more and ever more of the procedure.

3.   After Jo-Jo climbed higher onto the counter, he pulled on the doors and looked for the candy, stretching but missing jars and boxes in the rear with bright colors that beckoned but hid farther and farther from his reach.

PRACTICE 9 (pages 76–77)

First Sentence Part

Model: As he ran away into the darkness,
First Imitation: When they fusted nearby in a zurner,
Second Imitation: As her arm whirled fast over the egg-whites,
Third Imitation: After Jo-Jo climbed higher onto the counter,

Second Sentence Part

Model: they repented of their weakness
First Imitation: he confrusticated about his nestings
Second Imitation: her face shifted toward the cookbook
Third Imitation: he pulled on the doors

Third Sentence Part

Model: and ran after him,
First Imitation: and purted about them,
Second Imitation: and stared at it,
Third Imitation: and looked for the candy,

Fourth Sentence Part

Model: swearing
First Imitation: smiling
Second Imitation: grimacing
Third Imitation: stretching

Fifth Sentence Part

Model: and throwing sticks and great balls of soft mud at the figure
First Imitation: and turling stews and red bleeps of wrinkled networks to the morm
Second Imitation: and expressing confusion and frustration over the third direction in the recipe
Third Imitation: but missing jars and boxes in the rear with bright colors

Sixth Sentence Part

Model: that screamed and ran faster and faster into the darkness.
First Imitation: who flurded and narred cranster and cranster over the frame.
Second Imitation: that listed and explained more and ever more of the procedure.
Third Imitation: that beckoned but hid farther and farther from his reach.

PRACTICE 10 (pages 77–78)

1. B
2. C
3. B

PRACTICE 11 (pages 78–79)

1. This sentence matches model #2 in Practice 10.
2. This sentence matches model #3 in Practice 10.
3. This sentence matches model #1 in Practice 10.

PRACTICE 13 (pages 81–82)

1. **Lying on the floor of the flat-car with the guns beside me under the canvas,** I was wet, cold, and very hungry.
2. The trail moved up the dry shale hillside, **avoiding rocks, dropping under clefts, climbing in and out of old water scars.**
3. There was a tattered man, **fouled with dust, blood, and powder stain from hair to shoes,** who trudged quietly at the youth's side.
4. I brought the boat up to the stone pier, and the barman pulled in the line, **coiling it on the bottom of the boat** and **hooking the spinner on the edge of the gunwale.**

PRACTICE 14 (pages 82–85)

A. A pile of new debris cluttered up the driveway, and the tenants, **gazing at the disgrace,** watched with heavy hearts.
B. The dog sat up, his mouth clenching the rolled newspaper, **wagging his tail,** and begged a reward.
C. The upholstered pieces, the expensive, polished tables had been moved into the huge dining room, **covered with endless painter's cloths so that they would be protected from the splatterings of paint.**
D. The meeting that had been like a marathon among meetings continued, and the leader deliberated about his strategy, **stalling after the last remarks from the representative with whom he had planned so many emergency ploys focusing upon every conceivable tactic for the suppression of the opposition.**

PRACTICE 15 (pages 85–86)

1. **Bleeding profusely** and **cut off from his supply of eagles' blood,** he had never been closer to death.
2. The trail moved up the dry shale hillside, **avoiding rocks, dropping under clefts, climbing in and out of old water scars.**
3. He accepted new environment and circumstance with great coolness, **eating from his haversack at every opportunity.**
4. The farm building huddled like the clinging aphids on the mountain skirts, **crouched low to the ground as though the wind might blow them into the sea.**

5.   His face was fleshy and pallid, **touched with colour only at the thick hanging lobes of his ears and at the wide wings of his nose.**

6.   I pulled, raised, leaned forward, found the water, dipped and pulled, **rowing as easily as I could.**

7.   By and by, one group after another came straggling back to the mouth of the cave, **panting,** hilarious, **smeared from head to foot with tallow drippings, daubed with clay,** and **entirely delighted with the success of the day.**

8.   Adolph Knipe took a sip of stout, **tasting the malty-bitter flavor, feeling the trickle of cold liquid as it traveled down his throat and settled in the top of his stomach,** cool at first, **then spreading** and **becoming warm, making a little area of warmness inside him.**

PRACTICE 16 (pages 87–88)

1.   It was early in April in the year '83 that I woke one morning to find Sherlock Holmes standing, **fully dressed,** by the side of my bed.

2.   Presently the dawn began to break, and the sky to the east grew yellow and red, **slashed across with heavy black clouds.**

3.   The children crawled over the shelves and into the potato and onion bins, **twanging all the time in their sharp voices like cigar-box guitars.**

4.   And he, **sensing a new and strange and quite terrified note in all this the moment he read it,** at once looked over his shoulder at her and, **seeing her face so white and drawn,** signaled that he would meet her.

5.   In the late afternoon, the truck came back, **bumping and rattling through the dust,** and there was a layer of dust in the bed, and the hood was covered with dust, and the headlights were obscured with a red flour.

6.   He stood there, **balancing on one leg** and **holding tightly to the edges of the window sill with his hands,** staring at the sign and at the whitewashed lettering of the words.

7.   The people, **rushing forward,** waved and shrieked happily, **knocking down tables, swarming, rollicking, seizing the four Earth Men, lifting them swiftly to their shoulders.**

PRACTICE 17 (pages 88–89)

1.   Soon the men began to gather, **surveying their own children, speaking of planting and rain, tractors and taxes.**

2.   Flaherty even now was calling for his wife, **buying her a drink, filling whatever bar they were in with that voice of his and that easy laugh.**

3.   With the core of the reel showing, his heart feeling stopped with excitement, **leaning back against the current that mounted icily up his thighs,** Nick thumbed the reel hard with his left hand.

4. As she peered inside, with her legs apart and her hands on her knees, she whistled, unmelodically, through her teeth, **keeping time with a little uninhibited, pendulum action of her rear end.**

5. The train stopped in Vevey, then went on, **passing the lake on one side and on the other the wet brown fields and the bare woods and the wet houses.**

6. I stayed well out in the lake, **rowing awhile, then resting** and **holding the oars so that the wind struck the blades.**

7. Mrs. Carpenter was putting sun-tan oil on Sybil's shoulders, **spreading it down over the delicate, wing-like blades of her back.**

8. Lil, who would probably be just outside the gate with her boy, would hear Father's voice and hurry in, **knowing he would vent his rage on Mother,** and almost as soon as she entered the kitchen she would be greeted with a fist or a lifted boot, and soon her rouge and mascara would be mingled with tears and blood as she wilted under a cascade of senseless violence, **not knowing why she was being beaten, knowing only the blows and curses and enraged bellowings raining down on her.**

REVIEWING AND APPLYING
SENTENCE COMPOSING SKILLS

PRACTICE 1 (pages 90–91)

1. participle
2. appositive
3. participle
4. appositive
5. absolute
6. participle (past)
7. appositive
8. absolute

PRACTICE 2 (page 91)

1. participle
2. appositive
3. participle (past)
4. absolutes
5. absolutes
6. absolute
7. participle
8. participle (past)

9. appositive
10. appositives
11. participles
12. appositives

PRACTICE 8 (pages 99–100)

Note: Participles are present participles unless noted otherwise.

1. One participle, one absolute
2. One absolute, one participle
3. Two absolutes, one participle
4. One appositive, one absolute
5. One appositive, one absolute
6. Two absolutes, one participle
7. One absolute, one participle
8. Two participles, one past and the other present
9. One participle, two absolutes
10. Three participles, one present and the others past
11. One participle, one appositive
12. One participle, one absolute

PRACTICE 9 (pages 101–103)

1. **Standing on this limb,** you could by a prodigious effort jump far enough out into the river for safety. (present participle)

2. He began scrambling up the wooden pegs nailed to the side of the tree, **his back muscles working like a panther's.** (absolute)

3. Everyone shouted that Phineas must not be moved; someone else, **realizing that only a night nurse would be at the Infirmary,** did not waste time going there but rushed to bring Dr. Stanpole from his house. (present participle)

4. I washed the traces off me and then put on a pair of chocolate brown slacks, **a pair which Phineas had been particularly critical of when he wasn't wearing them,** and a blue flannel shirt. (appositive)

5. Shoving in his long bamboo poles, he pushed deliberately forward and slid slowly away from me down the gradual slope, **standing very upright, his skis far apart to guard against any threat to his balance, his poles sticking out on either side of him,** as though to ward off any interference. (present participle, two absolutes)

6. He was sitting on his cot, **elbows on knees, looking down.** (absolute, present participle)

7.   It was only that we could feel a deep and sincere difference between us and them, **a difference which everyone struggled with awkward fortitude to bridge.** (appositive)

8.   He trembled alone there in the middle of the park for hours, **wondering what would happen if he had an attack of appendicitis, unnerved by the thoughts of a fainting spell, horrified by the realization that he might have to move his bowels,** until at last we came. (present participle, two past participles)

9.   The ocean, **throwing up foaming sun-sprays across some nearby rocks,** was winter cold. (present participle)

10.   We left the party, **both of us feeling fine.** (absolute)

11.   We had dinner at a hot dog stand, with our backs to the ocean and its now cooler wind, **our faces toward the heat of the cooking range.** (absolute)

12.   To the right of them the gym meditated behind its gray walls, **the high, wide, oval-topped windows shining back at the sun.** (absolute)

13.   **Holding firmly to the trunk,** I took a step toward him, and then my knees bent, and I jounced the limb. (present participle)

14.   After about ten minutes he came walking rapidly out of his office, **his head down and his hands sunk in the pockets of his white smock.** (two absolutes)

15.   The sun was the blessing of the morning, **the one celebrating element, an aesthete with no purpose except to shed radiance.** (two appositives)

16.   The Devon faculty had never before experienced a student who combined a calm ignorance of the rules with a winning urge to be good, who seemed to love the school truly and deeply, and never more than when he was breaking the regulations, **a model boy who was most comfortable in the truant's corner.** (appositive)

17.   The tree was tremendous, **an irate, steely black steeple beside the river.** (appositive)

18.   I stood precariously in the middle of the room, **wanting desperately to leave and powerless to do so.** (present participle)

19.   The stadium itself, two white concrete banks of seats, was as powerful and alien to me as an Aztec ruin, **filled with the traces of vanished people and vanished rites, of supreme emotions and supreme tragedies.** (past participle)

20.   The advance guard which came down the street from the railroad station consisted of a number of Jeeps, **being driven with a certain restraint, their gyration-prone wheels inactive on these old ways which offered nothing bumpier than a few cobblestones.** (present participle, absolute)

21.   "What I like best about this tree," he said in that voice of his, **the equivalent in sound of a hypnotist's eyes,** "what I like is that it's such a cinch!" (appositive)

22. Finny got up, patted my head genially, and moved on across the field, **not deigning to glance around for my counterattack, but relying on his extrasensory ears, his ability to feel in the air someone coming on him from behind.** (two present participles)

23. The chocolate brown wicker furniture shot out menacing twigs, and three dozen of us stood tensely teetering our cups amid the wicker and leaves, **trying hard not to sound as inane in our conversation with the four present Masters and their wives as they sounded to us.** (present participle)

24. **Propped now before a great New England fireplace,** on this quiet old street, he looked like an invalid, house-bound. (past participle)

25. In class he generally sat slouched in his chair, **his alert face following the discussion with an expression of philosophical comprehension.** (absolute)

PRACTICE 10 (pages 103–104)

1. The ocean looked dead too, **dead gray waves hissing mordantly along the beach.** (absolute)

2. We spent an odd day, **toiling in that railroad yard.** (present participle)

3. I said nothing, **my mind exploring the new dimensions of isolation around me.** (absolute)

4. Others remembered that Phil Latham, **the wrestling coach,** lived just across the Common and that he was an expert in first aid. (appositive)

5. There they all were now, **the cream of the school, the lights and leaders of the senior class,** with their high I.Q.'s and expensive shoes, as Brinker had said, pasting each other with snowballs. (appositives)

6. The masters were in their places for the first Chapel, **seated in stalls in front of and at right angles to us, suggesting by their worn expressions and careless postures that they had never been away at all.** (past participle, present participle)

7. His talk rolled on, **ignoring and covering my look of shock and clumsiness.** (present participles)

8. We reached the others loitering around the base of the tree, and Phineas began exuberantly to throw off his clothes, **delighted by the fading glow of the day, the challenge of the tree, the competitive tension of all of us.** (past participle)

PRACTICE 11 (pages 104–105)

Note: Accept your sentence if it meets the following guidelines: (1) it adds either an absolute, an appositive, or a participle phrase of approximately the length indicated; and (2) it contains information that blends smoothly with the rest of the sentence.

1.   Finny, **his balance gone**, swung his head around to look at me for an instant with extreme interest, and then he tumbled sideways, broke through the little branches below, and hit the bank with a sickening, unnatural thud. (absolute)

2.   From my locker I collected my sneakers, jock strap, and gym pants, and then turned away, **leaving the door ajar for the first time.** ... (participle)

3.   It didn't seem fitting for Brinker Hadley, **the hub of the class**, to be congratulating me on influence. (appositive)

4.   First there was the local apple crop, **threatening to rot because the harvesters had all gone into the army or war factories**. (participle)

5.   With unthinking sureness I moved out on the limb and jumped into the river, **every trace of my fear of this forgotten.** (absolute)

6.   The windows now had the closed blankness of night, a deadened look about them, **a look of being blind or deaf.** (appositive)

7.   He came toward me, without his cane at the moment, **his new walking cast so much smaller and lighter that an ordinary person could have managed it with hardly a limp noticeable.** (absolute)

8.   **Looking back now across fifteen years**, I could see with great clarity the fear I had lived in, which must mean that in the interval I had succeeded in a very important undertaking: I must have made my escape from it. (participle)

PRACTICE 13 (pages 108–111)

A.   1. We found a stop watch in the office. 2. He mounted a starting box, leaned forward from the waist as he had seen racing swimmers do but never had occasion to do himself—I noticed a preparatory looseness coming into his shoulders and arms, a controlled ease about his stance which was unexpected in anyone trying to break a record. 3. I said, "On your mark—Go!" 4. There was a complex moment when his body uncoiled and shot forward with sudden metallic tension. 5. He planed up the pool, **his shoulders dominating the water while his legs and feet rode so low that I couldn't distinguish them**; a wake rippled hurriedly by him and then at the end of the pool his position broke; he relaxed, dived, an instant's confusion and then his suddenly and metallically tense body shot back toward the other end of the pool. 6. Another turn and up the pool again—I noticed no particular slackening of his pace—another turn, down the pool again, his hand touched the end, and he looked up at me with a composed, interested expression. 7. "Well, how did I do?" 8. I looked at the watch; he had broken A. Hopkins Parker's record by .7 second.

B.   1. The cat, unnoticed, had crept up on muffled paws from Zeena's seat to the table, and was stealthily elongating its body in the direction of the milk-jug, which stood between Ethan and Mattie. 2. The two leaned forward at the same moment, and their hands met on the handle of the jug. 3. Mattie's hand was underneath, and Ethan kept his clasped on it a moment longer than was necessary. 4. The cat, **profiting by this unusual demonstration**, tried to effect an unnoticed retreat, and in doing so backed into the pickle-dish, which fell to the floor with a crash.

C.   1. He was being looked at by a dead man who was seated with his back against a columnlike tree. 2. The corpse was dressed in a uniform that once had been blue, but was now faded to a melancholy shade of green. 3. The eyes, **staring at the youth**, had changed to the dull hue to be seen on the side of a dead fish. 4. The mouth was open. 5. Its red had changed to an appalling yellow. 6. Over the gray skin of the face ran little ants. 7. One was trundling some sort of a bundle along the lower lip.

D.   1. He dared not refuse, though the very thought of eating sickened him. 2. **Steeling himself against the first mouthful**, he dipped the spoon into the shimmering red liquid, lifted it to his lips. 3. Instead of reaching his mouth, the spoon reached only his chin, struck against the hollow under his lower lip, scalded it, fell from his nerveless fingers into the plate. 4. A red fountain splashed out in all directions, **staining his blouse, staining the white table cloth**. 5. With a feeling of terror David watched the crimson splotches on the cloth widen till they met each other.

E.   1. And while he debated, a loud, crashing noise burst on his ear. 2. At the same instant he received a stunning blow on the left side of the back, and from the point of impact felt a rush of flame through his flesh. 3. He sprang up in the air, but halfway to his feet collapsed. 4. His body crumpled in like a leaf withered in sudden heat, and he came down, **his chest across his pan of gold, his face in the dirt and rock, his legs tangled and twisted because of the restricted space at the bottom of the hole**. 5. His legs twitched convulsively several times. 6. His body was shaken as with a mighty ague. 7. There was a slow expansion of the lungs, accompanied by a deep sigh. 8. Then the air was slowly, very slowly, exhaled, and his body as slowly flattened itself down into inertness.

F.   1. There is a time in the life of every boy when he for the first time takes the backward view of life. 2. Perhaps that is the moment when he crosses the line into manhood. 3. The boy is walking through the street of his town. 4. He is thinking of the future and of the figure he will cut in the world. 5. Ambitions and regrets awake within him. 6. Suddenly something happens; he stops under a tree and waits as for a voice calling his name. 7. Ghosts of old things creep into his consciousness; the voices outside of himself whisper a message concerning the limitations of life. 8. From being quite sure of himself and his future he becomes not at all sure. 9. If he be an imaginative boy a door is torn open and for the first time he looks out upon the world, seeing, as though they marched in procession before him, the countless figures of men who before his time have come out of nothingness into the world, lived their lives and again disappeared into nothingness. 10. The sadness of sophistication has come to the boy. 11. With a little gasp he sees himself as merely a leaf blown by the wind through the streets of his village. 12. He knows that in spite of all the stout talk of his fellows he must live and die in uncertainty, **a thing blown by the winds, a thing destined like corn to wilt in the sun**. 13. He shivers and looks eagerly about. 14. The eighteen years he has lived seem but a moment, **a breathing space in the long march of humanity**. 15. Already he hears death calling. 16. With all his heart he wants to come close to some other human, touch someone with his hands, be touched by the hand of another. 17. If he prefers that the other be a woman, that is because he believes that a woman will be gentle, that she will understand. 18. He wants, most of all, understanding.